# Reach the Back Row

Creative Approaches for
High-Impact Preaching

By Murray Frick

Foreword by Leonard Sweet

Vital
**MINISTRY**
Loveland, Colorado

# REACH THE BACK ROW

Copyright © 1999 Group Publishing, Inc.

Visit our Web site: **www.grouppublishing.com**

## CREDITS
Editor: Dennis McLaughlin
Senior Editor: Dave Thornton
Chief Creative Officer: Joani Schultz
Copy Editor: Janis Sampson
Art Director: Kari K. Monson
Cover Art Director: Jeff A. Storm
Cover Designer: Fuller Creative, Inc.
Cover Photographer: Craig DeMartino
Illustrator: John McPherson
Computer Graphic Artist: Nighthawk Design
Production Manager: Peggy Naylor

## LIBRARY OF CONGRESS CATALOGING-IN-PUBLICATION DATA
Frick, Murray, 1954-
     Reach the back row : creative approaches for high-impact preaching
 / by Murray Frick ; with a foreword by Leonard Sweet.
       p.   cm.
     Includes bibliographical references.
     ISBN 0-7644-2126-3 (alk. paper)
     1. Preaching.  I. Title.
     BV4211.2.F745   1999
     251--dc21                        99-26382
                                         CIP

10 9 8 7 6 5 4 3 2 1       08 07 06 05 04 03 02 01 00 99

Printed in the United States of America.

# Acknowledgments

ACKNOWLEDGMENTS

There aren't enough pages to thank everyone who made it possible for me to put the words of this book down on paper.

My heartfelt thanks go out to

—those many congregational members who by their compassion and patience allowed me to practice my preaching skills over the years. Sometimes I failed in the pulpit and sometimes I succeeded, but whatever happened there were always many friends who continued to encourage me.

—Vera Hall, who continues to appreciate and support my efforts in bringing God's Word.

—my beloved wife, Susan, who has been a long-suffering companion on my many flights of imagination, and who still has the grace and humor to smile and shake her head when I come up with another "bright idea." God blessed me beyond knowing the day that Susan and I met.

—my daughters Erin, Ali, and Katie, who make a dad proud for knowing and celebrating the difference between being "childish" and "childlike," and for knowing who you are in spite of being PKs! Think of all the stories you'll have to tell your kids!

—and last, but never least, the Creator of all, who allows this sometimes prideful, sometimes uncertain, and usually unconventional preacher the privilege of speaking the good news.

God is indeed gracious and good in all things!

# About the author

AUTHOR

Dr. Murray Frick has been actively involved in professional ministry and preaching for over twenty years. He is currently the senior pastor of First Christian Church in Cheyenne, Wyoming, and holds a Doctor of Ministry Degree from Drew University. Dr. Frick also serves as technical director for the Cheyenne Little Theater and has been awarded several national and international honors for his work in theater.

# Contents

FOREWORD
# Foreword

---

T he early pioneers who provided the impetus for the Wesleyan movement that turned England and America upside down in the eighteenth and nineteenth centuries weren't as concerned about crafting pulpit masterpieces as they were with preaching sermons that hit the heart, changed lives, and changed the world.

When I finished reading Murray Frick's book, I thought I had been sitting at the feet of one of my on-fire Wesleyan ancestors. Frick has created a resource that will help preachers not just reach the front pews, where the cream of the crop convene, but actually *Reach the Back Row*.

Whenever I read the Gospels, I'm reminded again and again that Jesus prized the "common," especially the "common people" and the "common life." Jesus never lost the "common touch." It's difficult to escape the reality that Jesus did not speak to the crowds except in "performative utterances" called "parables" that were designed to bring about the very thing they were talking about.[1]

It's time we preachers reclaimed the "common touch." It's time preachers stopped spinning thread so fine, as Robert Burns once put it, that it is neither fit for weft nor woof. It's time preachers started communicating in ways that those within and without our stained-glass windows can hear and comprehend. Frick's book presents creative ways to do just this.

A recent poll asked Americans how they managed to escape "boredom" in their lives. Forty percent responded that they stayed away from church. That's how they purged boredom from their lives. One out of five adults admitted to daydreaming in church to alleviate boredom. Almost the same number (16.8 percent) simply *forced* themselves to pay attention, and 16 percent more checked out of the sermon by fixing their mind on solving problems at work and home or some other strategy.[2]

The post-Christian culture that we are currently experiencing is no longer urging people into churches. The church now has to go out into the world and convince people to come. What we are finding is that these postmoderns hear and learn things differently than the church is communicating them. Postmoderns are expressing their spirituality through images and metaphors, symbols and stories, body rituals and pilgrimages, but not through words.

For postmoderns, words get in the way of truth. The technology of a post-word world (TV, video, fax, e-mail, "surfing the Net") is displacing the Enlightenment culture of the book with a new visual and aural culture that is profoundly changing the home, the workplace, and the church. In this electronic culture, one recent University of Minnesota study indicates that visual aids increase persuasiveness by 40 percent.[3] No wonder the ultimate multisensory, multimedia art form is flourishing, while lots of other art forms are languishing.

Murray Frick does not offer any software explanations for his numerous killer apps. He did not intend this book to "search for new meaning in exegesis or as a critical analysis of God's Word." Furthermore, Frick writes, "You'll find no new proposals for word or linguistic studies." Yet Frick's method is based on an abductive postmodern hermeneutic that needs to be claimed and clarified.

Learning is not a linear movement either from (deduction) or towards (induction) propositions. Knowing proceeds through imaginative leaps, loops, and lurches that come to life almost holographically around performative metaphors. Philosopher Charles Sanders Pierce, who some have called the American Aristotle, insisted that faith in God comes not inductively or deductively, but abductively as the beauty of God opens in the believer an act of faith.[4] Pierce also argued that the first person in history who understood and employed the "abductive method" was Jesus of Nazareth.

While not explicating or exegeting abductive homiletics, Frick offers preachers some techniques to craft new narratives, or what I call EPIC (Experiential, Participatory, Image-based, Communal) Narratives.[5] Narratives that move postmodern learners from knowing God with our left brain to knowing God with our whole brain; from faith formation through catechism to faith formation through proverbs, stories, metaphors, music, images; from teaching through lecturers to teaching through artists, mentors, coaches, directors.

Frick is gentle with us at first. He lifts us up to the high wire slowly. He starts with the more safe active experiences like dramatic monologues, dialogues ("duet sermons"), and "letters from home." Then he moves us to riskier, karaoke preaching or what he calls "without-a-net" presentations of "brown bag sermons," "congregational conversations," mediated sermons, pageants, and other creative forms of communication.

What Frick never does is lift us up to let us down. The worst epitaph in existence is this German one: *Sie versprachen viel* ("They promised a lot.").

Frick delivers what he promises: practical, easy-to-use ideas for making your sermons come alive for this new day.

**Leonard Sweet**
President, SpiritVenture Ministries

# INTRODUCTION
# Introduction

Although it may be an unusual place to begin, let me tell you what this book is not. It isn't a book on theology. Wiser heads than mine have spent countless hours expounding on the marvels of God. Some of it is refreshing, some oppressive, some mystifying. But with the myriad of resources that already explore the depths of theological speculation, the focus of this book is elsewhere.

Neither is this book one that searches for new meaning in exegesis or the critical analysis of God's Word. You'll find no new proposals for word or linguistic studies. You'll discover no new radical insights into gospel interpretation. Yes, the art of exegesis is a complex and demanding discipline, and for most preachers it is the work and study of a lifetime; but it is another task for another writer.

Neither is this a book on preaching, at least in the traditional sense. The classic preachers, both historic and contemporary, are beyond my own abilities to present a compendium on preaching. Numerous existing volumes explore the depths of homiletic structure, style, and organization.[1] From the classic collections of notable preachers to scholarly presentations and fiery evangelists, the array of preaching material is endless.

So, you are probably wondering, what exactly is this book about? Simply this—it's about creatively communicating the Bible story.

With the constant demands placed on the shoulders of the contemporary pastor, it's easy to become lost in a world of obligation and commitment and forget why we preach. We don't preach because it's our job. We don't preach to impress people. We don't preach to entertain. We preach to draw our listeners into God's Word, if for only a moment, that God's grace might be revealed in their lives. We preach to invite listeners to encounter God's Word so they themselves become the light of that Word.

Thus you have the intent of *Reach the Back Row: Creative Approaches to High-Impact Preaching*. It's a book designed to help you extend traditional preaching into new regions. Its methods are intended to enhance the traditional sermon, not to replace it. The traditional sermon has a marvelous history and an important place in the life of the church. Whether it is cognitive or emotive, down home or formal, God's Word spoken from the pulpit, in its finest moments, is life changing. A sermon has the capacity to move us, instruct us, direct us, convict us, and console us. However, as every preacher knows, it can also be an exercise in boredom, triviality, and a hodgepodge of poorly organized ideas.

Hopefully, as you read through the pages of this book, you will be inspired to incorporate some new approaches into your preaching. As you do, you will release the conditioned ears of your congregation to hear God's Word in a way they've never heard it before.

Hopefully, each chapter will create in you a new passion for actively involving the people of your congregation in God's Word—even those seated in *the back row*. As you adapt these approaches to your own personal preaching style and unique congregational setting, you'll notice your preaching move from respectable to *high impact*. What's more, you can be assured that your congregation will notice.

On the practical level, this book begins with an overview of the different ways that people learn and what it means for the preacher. The book then presents seven primary approaches to preparing and presenting creative sermons and also includes a chapter containing several other odds and ends that can be easily adapted and used. Finally, chapter 10 presents some logistical considerations that will help increase the effectiveness of a sermon presentation.

Each approach presented in this book allows for a variety of development opportunities and personalization. Some of the ideas may spark your imagination into still other forms of creative communication. That's certainly part of its intent.

Crafting a sermon in one of these styles frequently takes more time than preparing one in a more traditional format. However, as a preacher who struggles each week to creatively engage people in God's Word, I've found that the response of the congregation is always positive. If I could respond to their spoken wishes, I would prepare my sermons from one of these forms every week.

Now that I've introduced the book, all that remains is for you to read it, pick one of the approaches, and use it to invite listeners to encounter God's Word in such a way that they themselves become the light of that Word.

So, no theology, no exegesis, no homiletics—just a few powerful and creative approaches to communicate the Bible story!

# CHAPTER 1
# Hearing, Seeing, and Touching the Sermon

# DIFFERENCES IN LEARNING

Although there are countless books that present a variety of models for learning and communication, most of them agree that all people speak, listen, and process information differently. This has some interesting implications for the preacher because it suggests there is potential for a mismatch between presentation style and learning style. If, for example, a preacher's typical mode of presentation is audible (as in the traditional sermon), but the audience is made up of visual learners, there is significant potential for fragmented communication between the preacher and the congregation. For a conscientious pastor, this implies that to effectively reach a majority of the congregation, he or she must develop sermons based on a variety of presentation styles and learning experiences. This may sound like a much more difficult charge than it actually is. Once a preacher becomes familiar with the different ways people learn and process information, sermon development is no more difficult than it is otherwise. In other words, by spending a little time becoming familiar with the process of learning, a preacher can maximize sermon outcome without increasing time spent in preparation.

At the risk of oversimplifying the learning process, people learn in one of three major ways: visually, (by what they see), audibly (by what they hear), or kinesthetically (by what they touch). Although people naturally learn through a combination of all three processes, most people have a predominant learning style. What this typically means for the lecture-style sermon is that the audible learners pay close attention and get the whole message, while people whose learning needs are predominantly visual or kinesthetic aren't getting it. And it's generally quite easy to identify the ones who aren't getting it. They're the ones whose faces are sporting the blank expressions. Typically, visual or kinesthetic learners get very little from a traditional lecture-style sermon, unless all three learning processes have purposely been built into it.

*Most people have a predominant learning style. What this typically means for the lecture-style sermon is that the audible learners pay close attention and get the whole message, while people whose learning needs are predominantly visual or kinesthetic aren't getting it. And it's generally quite easy to identify the ones who aren't getting it. They're the ones whose faces are sporting the blank expressions.*

In a given congregation, the *visual* learner may love the movements of the worship, whereas the *auditory* learner may be interested only in the music or spoken word. The *kinesthetic* learner, on the other hand, may want to get up and move during the sermon. Just as visual learners are interested in something more than a speaker who is rigidly locked to the sides of the pulpit, auditory learners don't care as long as they can hear every word and every nuance.

An important point to recognize is that if members of a congregation are listless or bored when listening to a sermon, it may have nothing to do with the presentation itself. More likely it indicates that the preacher is using a single style of communication and connecting with only a few listeners.

# Auditory Learners

In the average congregation, it is possible to see the drama of communicating and learning being acted out in practical ways. For example, those who learn best through the auditory mode (the listeners) often sit in the middle of the worship area so they can hear everything in detail—the music, the spoken word, the prayers, and the children's sermon. Every syllable, every nuance, every inflection is important. These listeners need to hear *everything* for the message to carry its full meaning. These folks are often content with a drab, uninteresting sanctuary and couldn't care less about the paint color or the furnishings. First and foremost, they listen.

Auditory learners respond to preaching that paints a picture with words. The careful crafting of sermons that touch the imagination through the precise use of the language speaks most effectively to them. Use, for example, the setting of a cabin in the woods. Auditory processors prefer to hear about a cabin that "was everything the city house was not—rustic, old, threatening imminent collapse—and filled with the smells of dust, mold, and grandma's sachets." With the use of a few extra words and a bit of mental imaging, the cabin has become more than a simple building in the woods. It has taken on a unique existence of its own. These few words allow the auditory processors to enter into the experience in a way that is meaningful to them.

It's interesting to note that many auditory learners prefer to listen to a book recorded on tape than to view a movie. For these learners, listening to a story represents the best of both worlds. They experience listening to the book itself as well as the freedom to build images far richer, at least for them, than those seen on the screen. Also, auditory processors respond most effectively to verbal instructions and descriptions. If for example, a new procedure for taking Communion is to be incorporated into the worship service, auditory learners need to have the instructions explained in detail.

*Auditory learners respond to preaching that paints a picture with words. The careful crafting of sermons that touch the imagination through the precise use of language speaks most effectively to them.*

# Visual Learners

Next there are the visual learners (the watchers) who often sit in the back of the worship area (or the balcony) so they can see the big picture—the movements of the service, from the sitting and standing of participants to the movement of people on the worship platform. They are drawn, not only by the spoken words, but also by the movement and progression of worship as it moves from beginning to end. These are the people who are literally drawn into a sermon by their eyes. Every visual detail communicates to them—the colors, the textures, the light, and the shadows. Visual learners listen to the choir with their eyes. A grimace on the face of a choir member will convey a mistake that their ears would never hear. The visual processors are those who, first and foremost, watch.

Visual learners need to be pulled into the sermon using "visual aids." The static presentation of a story presents difficulties for them. Even the simplest movements provide a key for reaching them. The visual processor can best be brought into a sermon by the body language of the preacher. An illustration about a baseball player stepping up to the plate and swinging the bat will be much more powerful if it becomes a description of action they can actually see. In other words, as the preacher describes someone stepping up to home plate, he or she can go through the movements at the same time. Have you ever noticed that children model this teaching style very well? Children often accompany their explanations with *play-by-play* actions. Together their words and actions give the fullness of an experience. In the same way, visual processors enter into the fullness of the experience when they are given the opportunity to see movement and action.

*Visual learners need to be pulled into the sermon using "visual aids." The static presentation of a story presents difficulties for them. Even the simplest movements provide a key for reaching them.*

# Kinesthetic Learners

Finally, there are the kinesthetic learners (the movers), who often sit in the front seats of the worship area. These learners need to be drawn into the experience by participating in a physical way. Kinesthetic learners want to move with the music, share something with the person next to them, shake the hands of other worshippers, move to the front to take Communion, and do anything else that keeps them physically active in the service. What kinesthetic learners hear is important; what they see is nice; but to fully involve them in a sermon, they must be allowed to participate physically.

For kinesthetic learners, opportunities to participate in the worship experience—engaging their bodies as well as their minds—will always be welcomed. The members of the congregation who excel in athletics, dance, carpentry, or even surgery are likely to have a dominant kinesthetic learning style. In order to fully engage these learners in the message, the skilled preacher will tap their talents for drama and liturgical dance. For those who are hesitant to participate from the platform, lead them to use hand motions or body postures during prayer and praise. Encouraging the congregation to kneel, bow, or raise its hands in worship are all effective ways to engage kinesthetic learners.

*For kinesthetic learners, opportunities to participate in the worship experience—engaging their bodies as well as their minds—will always be welcomed.*

Every congregation has a unique blend of individuals that represent all three learning styles. If a preacher presents every sermon in the form of a lecture, he or she will inadvertently give an advantage to the audible listeners at the expense of the visual and kinesthetic.

In one way each congregation is like a fingerprint—no two are the same. But unlike a fingerprint, the makeup of the congregation changes throughout the years.

This is important to take note of for the simple reason that because a method of preaching worked ten years ago doesn't mean it will have the same impact today. There are several reasons for this, but one of the most influential is exposure. The quality and use of media have changed so drastically in our culture that people are conditioned to learn differently than they did just ten years ago. This is not a cultural judgment, but rather a fact that needs to be acknowledged as preachers make strides to effectively communicate God's Word. Media is successful at reaching many individuals for a single reason: It creates a whole experience.

> *The quality and use of media have changed so drastically in our culture that people are conditioned to learn differently than they did just ten years ago. This is not a cultural judgment, but rather a fact that needs to be acknowledged as preachers make strides to effectively communicate God's Word.*

# CREATING A TOTAL LEARNING EXPERIENCE

Those of us who have been charged with communicating the Word of God can learn a great lesson from the contemporary media scene—the key to filling the gap created by differing learning needs is to turn the sermon into a total learning experience. Turning the sermon into a total experience is important on two levels. First, this type of sermon will appeal to and reach a wide variety of listeners, no matter what their predominant learning styles. And second, the sermon itself becomes an actual *experience*. Learning through experience is the best possible way to learn the lessons of life. As you think back on your own life, you'll undoubtedly discover that your most significant life-changing lessons didn't come through listening to a lecture or from reading something in a book. Rather, the life-changing experiences probably came through the experiences themselves, whether they were positive or negative. People who learn through experience retain the knowledge much longer and incorporate it into their life more effectively than those who are exposed to one-dimensional learning activities. To be three-dimensional, a sermon needs to include elements that appeal to visual, auditory, and kinesthetic learners. There are many approaches that a preacher can use to turn the sermon into a total learning experience, several of which will be discussed in subsequent chapters.

In case you might think that using a creative three-dimensional approach in a sermon is new or improper, go back and reread the classic book on communication—the Bible. As you do, you'll find examples of dramatic storytelling, dialogue, letters, object lessons, and emotionally powerful stories. Jesus himself used a variety of learning experiences to teach people around him. He drew in the sand, pointed to a withered tree, held up a coin, welcomed children to his side, and washed his disciples' feet. Using ideas that appeal to a variety of learning needs isn't really new at all, and it's certainly not improper. It's just that many of us have forgotten how to create true learning experiences that engage our listeners in the fullness of God's Word.

> *In case you might think that using a creative three-dimensional approach in a sermon is new or improper, go back and reread the classic book on communication—the Bible. As you do, you'll find examples of dramatic storytelling, dialogue, letters, object lessons, and emotionally powerful stories.*

# A FINAL NOTE

Several years ago while attending a master's workshop in choral conducting, I was struck by how preaching and directing a musical ensemble are very much alike. During the workshop I heard this statement that has had a significant impact on my preaching: "It's the conductor's job to communicate everything the performers need to know. If they fail to understand, most likely it's because the conductor has failed to communicate. More words won't solve the problem; conductors must make better use of their skills to accurately and precisely communicate."

This statement holds significant truth for us as preachers of God's Word. It's the preacher's job to communicate everything the listeners need to know. If individuals fail to understand, most likely it's because the preachers have failed to communicate effectively. More words seldom clarify. Very few individuals will understand the message any better after a bad forty-five-minute sermon than after a bad twenty-minute sermon. Louder or softer words may help to catch and hold attention, but they don't bring insight by themselves. The question then becomes, How do we communicate in a way that will engage the congregation in God's Word?

*More words seldom clarify. Very few individuals will understand the message any better after a bad forty-five-minute sermon than after a bad twenty-minute sermon.*

Thus I invite you into the following chapters. The approaches, if put to use, will help turn your sermon into an active learning experience. The approaches are three-dimensional and are sensitive to all three styles of learning—a bit of costume here and a bit of movement there to create a visual picture; a brief insight into the life and passion of a Bible character to create an emotional tie-in; an interesting dialogue or a Letter From Home to challenge listening ears. Each approach provides a new, or at least different, learning opportunity for those who have gathered to hear God's Word. Each approach seeks to engage listeners in a way that God's grace might be revealed in their lives.

PASTOR BURNBAUM HAD ENDURED SNORING DURING HIS SERMONS IN THE PAST, BUT NEVER FROM HIS OWN WIFE.

# CHAPTER 2

# The Dramatic Monologue

# TELLING THE STORY

The Dramatic Monologue, or first-person narrative, is an exciting opportunity to engage listeners in the life of a Bible character or a historical Christian figure. In this type of sermon, the preacher plays the role of the Bible character and speaks to the congregation as that character. This type of sermon can take almost any form and be from a variety of perspectives. It might be Peter's view of his attempt to walk to Jesus on the water, Simon of Cyrene's thoughts as he carried the cross for Jesus, or Hannah's bittersweet emotions as she dedicated her baby in the temple. The Dramatic Monologue might also take the form of a historical Christian figure such as Martin Luther nailing up the Ninety-Five Theses in Wittenberg or John Huss as he was preparing to be led out and burned at the stake. It's easy to dismiss biblical characters and historical Christian figures as people from far-away times and places with different motives and cultures, and who had such different lifestyles that their lives have no relevance for us today. However, as detailed studies and comparisons illustrate, we have much more in common with the historical figures of our faith than we often realize.

> *The challenge in preparing and presenting a sermon in the form of a first-person narrative is in conveying the similarities of the historical situation to contemporary living. In a sense the listeners should feel as though the story is about them.*

The challenge in preparing and presenting a sermon in the form of a first-person narrative is in conveying the similarities of the historical situation to contemporary living. In a sense the listeners should feel as though the story is about them. Developing common ground between the character and the listeners is the foundation for this type of sermon. Although the details may change, the relationships, the search for meaning, and the quest for God's Word are similar. How many busy CEOs or entrepreneurs will have a new appreciation for Elijah suffering from a classic case of burnout? A success in every sense of the word, Elijah was a man of God who fought one-too-many battles, faced one-too-many challenges, and was ready to give up. Elijah ran away, in no particular direction, other than the fact it was simply *away*. Many people today can identify with Elijah's feelings of overwhelming helplessness. These are people who have given all they have to give and are now at the end of their wits, patience, and resources. What can they learn as they listen to "Elijah" recount his own difficulties and his road to renewal? What insight might listeners gain by simply realizing that stress and its associated feelings of helplessness point to the human need for renewal of body and spirit?

How many young adults will identify with the shock, the embarrassment, and the resolve of a young man who discovers that his wife-to-be has become pregnant—and with someone else's child? How would listeners respond today if a young girl claimed the child she bore came from God, that she had never had relations with any man, and that she was still innocent and pure? Would there be many people who would blame Joseph for feeling doubt and wanting to question Mary about the pregnancy? What can we learn about Joseph, the miraculous birth, and ourselves if we had just a few moments to peek inside and hear his most private thoughts? How much more closely would we identify with Mary if we were allowed to share her hopes and fears, her confusion and feelings of rejection as an unwed mother? How might these experiences change our approaches to caring for the expecting young women and single mothers in our communities?

*The Dramatic Monologue provides the speaker an opportunity to explore the thoughts, feelings, reactions, and convictions of a character.*

The Dramatic Monologue provides the speaker an opportunity to explore the thoughts, feelings, reactions, and convictions of a character. A speaker who presents this type of sermon can take on almost any role and tell the story as if it were actually occurring or as a memory of past events. From a biblical character to a spectator witnessing an event, a character portrayal is limited only by one's imagination.

It's important to note that the use of imagination in a sermon should never infringe upon the truths of Scripture. Imagination should be limited to creative preparation and presentation. This does not mean that speculation about the thoughts and emotions of a Bible character is out of bounds. Part of understanding God's Word comes from pondering its deeper meanings and trying to step into the experiences of the characters.

# CHOOSING YOUR CHARACTER

Choosing a character for a Dramatic Monologue is a matter of finding someone you want to portray and then allowing your listeners to see through you and into the life of the character. The object is to allow listeners to identify with a character and be given the opportunity to gain new insights into their own lives.

> *Choosing a character for a Dramatic Monologue is a matter of finding someone you want to portray and then allowing your listeners to see through you and into the life of the character.*

The easiest stories to develop are the well-documented lives of men and women in the Bible. Many Bible heroines, while often overlooked in developing character portrayals, can provide exceptionally colorful stories of faith.[2] As we listen to these women, we discover that their lives are not very different from our own. In many ways they are similar to the women in our families and in our congregations. What was Martha thinking? How was she feeling? What was driving her just before the confrontation with her sister Mary in the presence of Jesus? Was it sibling rivalry? Or was it the actions of an older sister who took pride in her skills as a hostess and in providing for the Master?

Or how about Eve, a woman who experienced the pain and turmoil of knowing that her firstborn son murdered his brother? We can imagine this first mother experiencing all the anxieties and torments suffered by other mothers. How would she tell her story? How is it like a story of today?

There are many Bible heroes who provide wonderful opportunities for character portrayals as well. For instance, what was going on in young David's head when he summoned his courage, ignored the whispers of his friends, and went out to face Goliath? Can you imagine him being slightly nervous? Did he feel anxiety for himself and for his own safety? Or did he have contempt for his brothers, who failed to place their faith in God?

Or consider Peter, a man who seemed to blurt out the most amazing things at the most amazing times. Did you ever think about why he talked of building "three shelters" at the Transfiguration? How is that like many of our own experiences when we've said something simply because we didn't know what else to say? How often have we wanted to pull back the words while they were in midair? What did Peter say for himself, probably under his breath, after his comment? "Open mouth, insert foot" is not a new concept, nor was it in Bible times. What can Peter teach us about ourselves by telling us his life story?

Personally, the stories I enjoy using most for character portrayals are the ones about the men and women who stand in the shadows and witness great events. Some of these individuals include the Bethlehem innkeeper, the unjust judge, and the master's steward. Other characters can be created by the preacher, drawing on personal life experiences and his or her own imagination. For example, the story of a woman who cooked the Passover meal for her Master and then witnessed the Last Supper, seeing what the disciples could not see. Or the story of a woman who hears about a man at the public well from her Samaritan sister.

*There are many Bible heroes who provide wonderful opportunities for character portrayals as well. For instance, what was going on in young David's head when he summoned his courage, ignored the whispers of his friends, and went out to face Goliath? Can you imagine him being slightly nervous? Did he feel anxiety for himself and for his own safety? Or did he have contempt for his brothers, who failed to place their faith in God?*

# DEVELOPING YOUR CHARACTER

Once a story is chosen, developing a character begins with both study and reflection. It requires blending the life of a particular individual with your own unique personal experiences.

A good place to begin preparation for the Dramatic Monologue is by asking a series of questions about the character you are developing. Use the "Character Development Work Sheet" (pp. 27-28) to help you get started.

# CHARACTER DEVELOPMENT WORK SHEET

························································································

• What events have happened (real or imagined) to shape this person's life?

_____

_____

• What does this person do for a living, and what unique skills might he or she have as a result?

_____

_____

• What faith, if any, does this person have?

_____

_____

• How is he or she related to the other characters and to the action of the story?

_____

_____

• How much of the story did the character know or witness?

_____

_____

• What are the general character traits of this person?

_____

_____

_____

• How old is your character?

_____

_____

• How well educated is this person?

_____

_____

• What does she or he look like physically?

_____

_____

_____

• How does he or she dress?

_____

_____

_____

• Is there anything unusual about this person's upbringing?

_____

_____

_____

• Is there anything that would make your character stand out in a crowd?

_____

_____

_____

• What facts, if any, do we know about this individual's character from biblical accounts?

_____

_____

_____

• What is the primary message this character should impart to the listeners?

_____

_____

_____

There are some practical things to consider when developing your character. For example, it is somewhat difficult for a woman to play the role of a male Bible character. She could, however, develop a convincing character as his wife or daughter, and then tell the story from that unique perspective. In the same manner, it is difficult for an older man to play a young boy. Although an older man could tell a story from his youth, perhaps as a dying man on his deathbed or as a feeble man sitting on a bench, reflecting on his past.

A female preacher might not want to play the part of a woman of ill repute, especially in church. It is possible, however, for a woman living in Sychar to tell us what she saw when one of *those* women had contact with Jesus. The story might be a wonderful account of repentance, or it might be given in the form of gossip. The character can be in awe or just matter-of-fact about the whole thing. The possibilities are limitless! The Bible gives us a wonderful tapestry of people and their lives. All we need to do is give them an opportunity to share their lives through us.

Once you've chosen a character and developed a background, it's time to go to work on the script. Whether it's a full script, an elaborate outline, or simply points to touch on along the way, the most successful monologues are those that are well prepared. The script in a sense is like a story. It should help the listener hear what the character hears, see what the character sees, and feel what the character feels. The best scripts are those that are broad enough to engage listeners in the life of the character, but with a precise focus that demands a response from each listener.

There are some preachers who are blessed with quick and accurate memories and find the memorization of a full script a quick and simple task. I, however, am not one of them! My memory is like a sieve; given enough time, anything can and will run through it. Consequently, I use either an outline that will cover the highlights, or I find a way to *cheat!* For example, when I portrayed Joseph in his carpenter's shop, I used a table I was *finishing* as a prop. The table was slightly tilted away from the congregation and had a copy of the script taped firmly to it. In addition, I used boldfaced headers, $1\frac{1}{2}$ line spacing for easy reading, and highlighted the beginning of each section; thus I was prepared to cheat in style!

# SETTING THE SCENE

Although a scenic background is not necessary for an effective monologue sermon, a few well-chosen props can add a great deal to its success. For example, if the character you are portraying is Joseph, a table to polish or a bit of woodwork will not only fit the character but also add to the effectiveness of the message. The character of Elijah, on the other hand, might have a staff and rucksack, the bare necessities of a man traveling in the wilderness. The woman at the well may carry a pot for water; while a shepherd may have a crook, a sling, and perhaps a pouch of pebbles. The character of an elderly man may sit on a bench, reminiscing about the past as he rests from the heat of the day. From his perch he is free to tell his stories of yesterday and today, sharing his own personal narrative and hard-won wisdom with all who will listen.

*The use of props and costumes in a sermon helps to create a visual image that is different from the typical pulpit presence. Props are even more effective if they require movement, which is an important part of communicating, especially for visual learners.*

Costuming is another important consideration when developing a character portrayal. Costumes can add a powerful dimension to the sermon and be designed with little effort. Although elaborate costumes may have a wonderful effect, they are not always practical or affordable. The simplest "costume" such as a robe and bare feet is usually sufficient to move the congregation to a different time and place. Keeping the costume simple will also help the worship service flow in the least interrupted manner. In addition, the simpler the costume the easier the transition from the here and now to the past. The pause that occurs when the speaker changes into costume can actually help prepare the congregation to go on the journey with you.

The use of costuming and props will definitely add seasoning to any sermon. The simple use of a robe and skullcap along with a polishing rag and rough table, quickly transforms the preacher into Joseph ready to tell us his story. The same robe, a rope belt, a headband, and a long piece of cord to be knotted, and Alaias the sailor is ready to share the tale of Paul's shipwreck or the journey of a reluctant prophet who was swallowed whole! Provide a robe, head covering, and needle with thread, and Mary can tell about her wonder at the angel's visit. Replace the needle and thread with a jar, and Mary's character becomes the woman who desperately seeks Jesus' forgiveness at Simon's house. Add items such as pottery dishes or trays, and the woman can be Mary or Martha. Choose instead a ledger and pen and the character becomes Priscilla, a key leader in the young church.

Although very simple, these additions can help the congregation move out of today and into a different world. The use of props and costumes in a sermon helps to create a visual image that is different from the typical pulpit presence. Props are even more effective if they require movement, which is an important part of communicating, especially for visual learners.

> *The use of costuming and props will definitely add seasoning to any sermon. The simple use of a robe and a cap, a polishing rag and a rough table, and the preacher is quickly transformed into Joseph ready to tell us his story.*

Movement is another important dimension in the Dramatic Monologue. To be effective, the speaker should move away from the pulpit to engage listeners at a more personal level.

# DELIVERY

Arguably, the most important part of the monologue sermon is the delivery. As the speaker begins to portray a character, it is important for him or her to think as much like the character as possible. Ask yourself how you would respond in the same situation. How fast do you think when you're trying to wrestle with thoughts or emotions that are life changing? If you were to speak those thoughts aloud, how rational would they sound? Would they be delivered in rapid fire, or would they ramble around in incomplete sentences?

The way a speaker portrays emotions is also an important element in sermon delivery. The more the delivery looks, sounds, and feels like real life, the easier it will be for listeners to believe in the character. For example, anger is a quick, loud emotion delivered in a high-pitched voice, similar to fear. Reflection, on the other hand, is slower in delivery and softer in volume.

*The way a speaker portrays emotions is also an important element in sermon delivery. The more the delivery looks, sounds, and feels like real life, the easier it will be for listeners to believe in the character.*

Another important consideration is the range of emotions that make up a character's experience. Is your character proud of his or her experience or embarrassed by it? Are the emotions consistent throughout the story, or do they change as the character relives them? How would you expect someone to act if they were experiencing the events firsthand? If you are able to find these feelings within yourself and accurately portray them, you will have an important key to delivering a believable character presentation. The more vulnerable a speaker becomes, the more easily the listeners can identify with the character he or she is portraying.

# Sample Monologue Sermon

## Introduction

The following Dramatic Monologue is the firsthand story of a man named Bartimeus. Bartimeus traditionally receives billing as an unnamed individual known simply as *the innkeeper*. The innkeeper is often painted as a scoundrel for not giving a room to young, pregnant Mary. This is his opportunity to tell the story from his own unique perspective.

The script was developed with the image of a married Bartimeus. He is the owner of an inn that he inherited from his father. Bartimeus, who is horribly overworked, is a very loving man but slightly *henpecked* by his wife. The events of the evening find him extremely busy with the overflowing crowds brought by the mandated census. Bartimeus would likely forget his own name if it weren't being *yelled* at him all the time. The scene takes place in the common room of his inn. Bartimeus is wearing a simple robe covered by an apron. His feet are bare, or perhaps he wears simple sandals. On his head he wears a yarmulke (the prayer cap worn by faithful Jews). His props consist of a towel and a stack of simple plates and mugs on a large tray that he will wipe "dry" during the course of the monologue. Bartimeus' narrative moves between *today* and the events of the past. Like anyone else recounting a story, he is occasionally interrupted with his life *now*.

# THE INNKEEPER'S STORY

*Bartimeus enters, puffing slightly, carrying a huge tray with clean mugs or bowls to be dried. He is obviously in no hurry to complete this task, as it gives him a much-needed break to share his story. He speaks with an accent that is foreign, but understandable (perhaps a light Yiddish, not so out of proportion as to become a parody).*

*(Bartimeus puts down some of his work and begins to address the congregation.)*

My name is Bartimeus. It's a good name, an honest name; one that's been in my family for generations. I have come to tell you my story. It's not an important story in the great picture of things, but Yahweh uses even the simplest tools to create his works, as my father used to say.

My father was a great teller of stories and shared many wonderful sayings, he did. He had a story for every occasion and was as wise as the wisest rabbi in Jerusalem, he was. And he was an honest businessman, building up his trade and treating people fairly.

But, I'm rattling on, as my Abital would say. She takes exception to my talking and sharing stories with our customers—says I talk too much and work too little. Of course, she is happiest when she is complaining or yelling at the help. *(Pause.)* And she is a happy woman!

I guess she's right, *(pause)* sometimes. When times are slow, and they often are when the trade routes are empty, I have time to stop and tell stories and to hear the news that comes from around the region. Sometimes it comes as far away as Joppa, Beersheba, or even Damascus!

But, when things are busy, I would most likely forget my name if the customers weren't yelling it at me day and night! One thing drives out another, as they say, and I'll forget what I'm doing and where I'm going. As my father used to say, "Busy hands have not time for the work of mischief." So I guess I should consider myself a lucky man.

You see, I run a small business. It's an inn, started by my father's father and handed down to me. I'm an honest businessman. I give fair measure for a fair price. My food is simple, but wholesome and filling. My cider and ale are mellow and served in clean ware. The rushes on the floor are changed regularly and even my smallest room is clean for the traveler who stays the night or the trader who stays the month.

Now, it's not a fancy place, mind you. "Handsome is as handsome does," as my father used to say. There are fancier places near the city's heart and imposing buildings near the city's gates, but we do all right, we do all right.

Then, of course, there are the Romans. I guess they aren't too bad around us. Oh, some of them don't like us. They see us as something less than people and treat us that way. And I have as little love for those who occupy our lands as anyone else. The common soldiers who desire drink and companionship usually go to other inns. We only host the occasional petty officer and his family, who are good enough.

But, here I go again—away from my story. "A full cup holds no more but drains out a little," as my father used to say. Now, where was I? Oh, yes, the inn—a good little inn, a place that I hope one day to pass to my son. That night actually started out in Rome. I say that because that's where the Caesar fellow lives. He decided that he wanted to know how many people lived in the whole of his kingdom. I really think he planned on raising taxes. "You don't trust the fox to guard the hen-house," as my father used to say.

Anyway, Caesar was determined to find out how many people lived where; so he sent everyone back to where their fathers' homes had been. Now you must understand that our town is but a small stop on the busy trade routes. But it is a part of David's house, and we're proud of that. You know David? The King? The REAL King? Not like this Caesar fellow! Oy vay, I could tell you stories about David!

*(Bartimeus responds to something only he can hear, from over his shoulder. It is his wife, calling him back to the task at hand.)*

What? OK, OK, I'll get back to my story! *(Bartimeus returns his attention to the audience.)* That was Abital, making herself happy… *(over his shoulder, to the same out-of-sight location)* BY YELLING!

Anyway, the order goes out, but the local officials can't begin to handle the flood of people who come in. It should have taken a day, two at the most. But a day turned into a week and there was still no end in sight. Other inns raised their rates—two, three, five times higher than their normal prices. But I saw no reason to cheat other Jews who had no choice but to wait.

So, as the week progressed, it became harder and harder to get decent food to prepare wholesome meals for my customers. Food that should have lasted until the next harvest started running low, and tempers began to flare. Every night, the people would sit and shout at me, "Bartimeus, get me drink!" "Bartimeus, get me food!" "Bartimeus…Bartimeus…Bartimeus!" Little wonder I would lose myself in the blur of every evening!

Now, even though it's been some time ago, I remember that one night as clearly as if it were yesterday!

The evening started like any other. People who were camping outside the city walls were looking for a meal; travelers who had been caught up in the madness of this event were looking for a place to spend the night; and beggars were looking for anything they could find. Oy vay, how many times would I receive a tongue-lashing from those I had to send away? But then, what was I to do? My rooms had been full for weeks. Even the benches in the common room were full each night with those who slept there because they had no other place to go.

And then there was a man at my door. I really didn't pay him much mind—I was far too busy. But when I looked up, he was just standing there. You could read the familiar story on his face. Like everyone else, he was looking for a place to stay. He must have tried every other place in the city before he ended up here. And as he looked around the common room it was obvious, even to him, my humble inn was beyond full and was bursting at the seams!

But, he came anyway. Asking for a place to stay, any place to stay. I could hardly hear his voice over the noise of the room, but I knew his story. I'd heard it a hundred times before. I was just about to turn him away when I saw his wife through the open door. The poor thing was no more than a child herself. She was riding a scruffy old donkey and was long overdue to bring a child into the world. Yet *(pause)* there was a wonderful kind of peace in her face; it was that special look that Yahweh gives to women in her condition.

I knew I couldn't turn them away. But there was just no place for them! And even though I knew Abital would have my head if she found out, I offered them room in the stable. Their beast would have to stay in the courtyard, there was just nowhere else for it. But the other beasts in the stable would be quite warm enough to ease the chill of the night. Besides the sweet smell of the hay would help cover the smell of the slop in the back alleyways.

From the look on the young man's face, you would have thought I had given him an inheritance! He thanked me, and then thanked me again! I sent my youngest son to help move the animals and throw out some fresh straw. I really didn't have time to think of them again that evening. I had customers waiting.

It was later that night, quite a long time later. The fire in the main hearth had died down, and the last of my customers had drifted off to their rooms or had fallen asleep on the benches of the common room. I was cleaning up the last of the crockery and tapping a new hogshead for the morrow when I first saw it. I thought it was my imagination at first. There shouldn't have been a light like that in the sky unless half the town was on fire! I ran out into the lane and saw a glow off beyond the hills.

Now, I know that area. I ran in those hills like every boy in my youth; there's nothing out there for miles in any direction except empty hills and sheep. Yet there was a glow as if the hills themselves were on fire! I did nothing but stare for a while. But then, I was deathly tired and knew it was long past time to find my own bed. It was wonderment, but a wonderment that was beyond me.

I turned to go back inside, but as I did, I noticed a commotion at the stable. At first I thought it was thieves. And if so, they would feel the sting of my stick on their backsides if I caught them.

*(Bartimeus shows his anger and directly addresses the congregation.)* Even in the midst of the hardships around us, I have no patience for thieves. I will help anyone willing to work, but I have no love for those that would steal from Jew or Gentile! Then I remembered the man and young girl with child. I'd forgotten them!

But now, it looked as though someone had set the stable on fire. If that couple had harmed my stable, I would turn them out, expecting or not! I burst in, either ready to provide a lashing to some thieves or to throw that couple out right then. But something stopped me short. It wasn't what was happening there that stopped me. It was what wasn't, if you can tell what I'm saying.

But then you'll probably think me a madman. There was no fire, no commotion, no sound; it was as if the earth was holding its breath. Even the animals had become so quiet. And there they were—the man and his wife, and a little baby whose age could be counted in moments. Now I've seen babies. And I have as soft a heart for them as any other. But let me tell you, this one seemed…different. I could hardly help myself. I stood and stared like the fool that I felt I was. And the woman looked up—and she smiled at me. She smiled as though she knew secrets that I could never begin to fathom. *(Pause.)* And my old stable looked like a royal court, holding its queen.

And then they came—down from the hills. At first by ones and twos, panting as if they had been running from a lion. Then more and more—shepherds! Some silent as the night, others crying and laughing! Some came to stare. Others came simply to kneel. But they came, crowding in to see this tiny baby! Some were talking of visions and voices; others spoke of angels. They were talking like the prophets of my great grandfather's time.

I don't know exactly what they were looking for. But I knew what I saw and felt. Yahweh himself was there! I don't know how I knew, but I knew. And I had given him a bed of straw!

Well, the night was wearing on, and the morning would come soon enough. Even in the splendor, I knew I must sneak away and get myself abed. I thought to check on the young couple in the midday. But then I was busy. By the time I did go to check on them, they were gone.

*(Bartimeus pauses, reflecting.)* My young son told me that they had settled their accounts and had gone away. How I wish I had taken a moment to ask them who they were and from where they had come. How I wish I had taken time to ask them what it all meant. I hope they remember me kindly.

*(Bartimeus abruptly returns to the present and looks over his shoulder.)* Ah, there's Abital again. She's come to scold me again about talking too much and working

too little. I must be on about my chores. I never did find out any more about that young family, but somehow I have a feeling that Yahweh has great things planned for them, great things indeed!

*(Bartimeus collects his things and leaves.)*

# Assessing the Story

If you take a few minutes to study "The Innkeeper's Story," you will see that it is three-dimensional and includes elements that appeal to all three learning styles. The narrative speaks to those who are auditory learners, whereas the costuming, props, and movement draw the visual learners into the story. All the elements working together with the emotions accurately portrayed by Bartimeus will engage those who are primarily kinesthetic learners.

The Dramatic Monologue, if done properly, provides a total learning experience that will immerse listeners in God's Word.

# Other Creative Ideas for Monologue Sermons

There are many other biblical characters whose lives lend themselves to the easy development of exciting and interesting Dramatic Monologues.

• **Young David preparing to face Goliath.** A simple costume for young David might include a simple robe belted at the waist, and sandals. A sling and a small pouch of stones are excellent hand props for a shepherd boy. While there are many approaches one could take with this character, a powerful story could be developed around David putting his faith to the test as he steps out to confront the giant.

• **Mary, the mother of Jesus, after the birth of Christ.** A costume for Mary might include a tunic worn beneath a longer robe, and sandals. A clean rag or two and a bench to sit on will suffice for props. The focus of the character's monologue might range from a review of the events of the past months to reflecting on Joseph's rage and his eventual acceptance of her pregnancy. Other ideas include her meeting with Elizabeth, the Annunciation, the demanding journey to Bethlehem, and the birth of the baby Jesus.

• **The adventures of Paul.** A ragged robe, belted at the waist, is all that is needed for Paul's costume. A simple bench and table, as well as pen and paper, will make excellent props. The focus of the Dramatic Monologue might be to allow the congregation to eavesdrop on the internal dialogue of an old man now imprisoned in Rome. It could also take the form of a brief reflection on the journey of life that led the arrogant young Saul to become the transformed Paul, a recount of the shipwreck, or the days of missionary travel that changed Paul's life forever.

• **Martha, sister of Mary.** Martha's costume might be an attractive robe with a shawl, either belted or tied back at the waist. Appropriate serving utensils and a tray or linen could be used for hand props. The character of Martha might tell the story of an older sister who worked hard to present a pleasant home for the Master's visit. In need of rest, she turned to Jesus to correct her sister Mary, but was instead corrected herself.

# CHAPTER 3

# The Dialogue Sermon

# TELLING THE STORY

Christians have a dubious history when it comes to hearing and discerning the voice of God in their midst. But what would happen if God interrupted the worship service and said exactly what was on his mind? There would probably be as many different reactions as there are members of the congregation. But certainly no one would argue about the power of the experience.

An interruption of this nature is the premise that sets the stage for the Dialogue Sermon. This type of sermon is simply a conversation that takes place between two speakers. For our purposes the dialogue takes the form of a conversation between the preacher and God.[3]

*Although a dialogue between God and the preacher can be developed into a very powerful sermon, it is flexible enough to be used in a variety of settings. If used as an opening devotion for a board or committee meeting, it can set the stage to help members focus on God's business rather than on personal agendas.*

Although a dialogue between God and the preacher can be developed into a very powerful sermon, it is flexible enough to be used in a variety of settings. If used as an opening devotion for a board or committee meeting, it can set the stage to help members focus on God's business rather than on personal agendas. It can be used at any point during the worship service. And although the dialogue takes place in a fixed location in the worship area, its setting can be developed using a variety of locations, such as the preacher's study, the preacher's home, in the doctor's office, in the grocery store, or anywhere else. Your imagination is the only limit. Since God is truly everywhere at once, there should be no surprise wherever we meet him.

The Dialogue Sermon provides an opportunity for the speaker to ask questions, seek insights, and simply allow the Bible to speak in a contemporary way. It's a creative way for God's Word to reach beyond the listeners' habitual defenses and listening habits. A well-crafted Dialogue Sermon is humorous, touching, insightful, and, above all, practical. It should deal with questions of real concern today, allowing God's timeless Word to be heard in a modern context.

# DEVELOPING THE SCRIPT

For a Dialogue Sermon to be effective, it requires (1) a setting with which the audience can identify; (2) a problem or situation that is familiar; and (3) a loving, authoritative voice for God's part.

The voice of God does not have to sound like Charlton Heston! You may even wish to choose a different person to read God's part each time you present a sermon of this type. Using a variety of people serves as a wonderful way to include several different congregation members. I happen to be blessed with a member of my congregation that allows me to converse with the same God "voice" whenever I present a Dialogue Sermon. Either way that works is appropriate.

> *A well-crafted Dialogue Sermon is humorous, touching, insightful, and, above all, practical. It should deal with questions of real concern today, allowing God's timeless Word to be heard in a modern context.*

The object of this sermon is to stage a simple conversation between the speaker and someone playing the voice of God. It should include no fancy words or King James English, nor be based on a strictly formal sentence structure.

The first time a conversation between God and the preacher occurs during a sermon, it will be natural for the preacher to act more than a bit skeptical. After all, how many preachers or listeners actually expect to have the worship service interrupted by God's voice?

The script should be developed in a manner that allows the speaker an opportunity to talk to God about current issues. These conversations can cover any subject that has importance in the life of the congregation. The most effective conversations tend to be a bit Socratic. In other words, with the helpful direction of God, the preacher stumbles toward his or her own conclusions. In a great display of ultimate wisdom, God might even choose to ignore certain questions asked by the preacher. In so doing, God's character can demonstrate his great wisdom and work beyond human agendas.

# SETTING THE SCENE

The setting for the dialogue can be as simple or as complex as you wish to make it. A folding chair and a small table will effectively serve as a living room, den, business office, or waiting room. A telephone, a stack of papers, the local newspaper, or a pile of mail will help create a familiar and realistic scene.

As with the Dramatic Monologue, a bit of costuming will add to the atmosphere. Slippers can make the setting look like home. Wearing an old work coat will help set the scene out-of-doors. A hand prop or two, depending on the focus of your message, will also lend a sense of realism.

*An effective and compelling sermon presentation involves practicing the script several times. Running through it ahead of time allows an opportunity to check the script's timing and word flow and also provides an overall familiarity with the dialogue. A few times through the script will make all the difference in the world in the final presentation!*

# DELIVERY

As in all creative sermons of this nature, memorization is wonderful, but not always practical. Hiding a copy of the script or developing one that leads you to natural responses will take the pressure off of trying to memorize it. If the preacher has thoroughly developed a clear direction for the dialogue, he or she should be able to avoid the use of a script and respond to God's voice with an appearance of spontaneity. Most preachers are fairly good at improvisation, and as long as they are sufficiently familiar with the thrust of the dialogue, memorization is not necessary.

The Dialogue Sermon is most effective if the individual reading the part of God is out of sight. A disembodied voice over the sound system works best. Be sure to prepare a complete script for the person speaking the part of God. The person can simply read the script and can also prompt the preacher should he or she manage to forget a line or two.

An effective and compelling sermon presentation involves practicing the script several times. Running through it ahead of time allows an opportunity to check the script's timing and word flow and also provides an overall familiarity with the dialogue. A rehearsal or two also allows the preacher an opportunity to see how well, or poorly, the material is recalled. As a result, he or she can make whatever notes are necessary to support the speaker's memory. A few times through the script will make all the difference in the world in the final presentation!

*The Dialogue Sermon provides the freedom to be straightforward with particular issues which, if spoken directly to the congregation, might otherwise cause defensive reactions. This freedom is one of the greatest strengths of the Dialogue Sermon.*

SAMPLE SERMON
# Sample Dialogue Sermon

## Introduction

The following Dialogue Sermon takes place between God and a typical preacher, who is burdened with an impossible schedule and the desire to be everything to everyone. The dialogue occurs at the end of a very busy day. Its relevance will be obvious to your congregation members because even the most faithful of God's workers find themselves spending too much time "doing" their faith and too little time "living" it.

# EXCUSE ME?

*The speaker collapses in a chair that is set near a table. On the table is a telephone, some papers, and a scheduling calendar. The only costuming consideration is the possible use of a short-sleeved shirt to help illustrate a preacher trying to relax after a busy day of ministry.*

**Preacher:** *(Collapsing in the chair)* Wow, what a day! I can't believe I have to go back to church tonight for another building-committee meeting. Thank God for a break! I am so tired! I've been looking forward to a few minutes off all day.

**God:** Hello, [name of preacher].

**Preacher:** *(Picking up phone)* Hello? Hello? Aargh…computerized sales…the phone rings and no one's there!

**God:** HELLO, [name of preacher].

**Preacher:** *(Loudly)* Enough! Can't a guy get a little peace and quiet? *(Looks at* *phone, puzzled.)*

**God:** HELLO, [name of preacher].

**Preacher:** Who said that?

**God:** I did.

**Preacher:** Uh-huh…(*Looks around carefully, under chair, table, papers.)* And just who are you?

**God:** I AM WHO I AM.

**Preacher:** And just who is that? Is this Doug? Is there a radio or something hidden in here? Is this your idea of a joke?

**God:** I told you who I AM.

**Preacher:** *(Still looking)* Yeah, right. This is cute, it's been fun, now knock it off! This is my only chance all day to rest. *(To self)* It's got to be one of my friends trying to pull a practical joke.

**God:** Do you really believe that?

**Preacher:** I know there's no one here… *(Loudly)* Is that you, [name of preacher's spouse]?

**God:** [Name of preacher's spouse] can't hear you. [Name of preacher's spouse] isn't home yet. It's just us.

**Preacher:** It's not just "us"; it's just "me"! It's finally happened—one too many board meetings—one too many budget conferences—one too many youth fellowship scavenger hunts. If I haven't "lost it," I've seriously misplaced it!

**God:** Do you really believe that?

**Preacher:** OK, who is this really? I'm starting to lose my patience!

**God:** I AM WHO I AM.

**Preacher:** Yeah, and I'm King David!

**God:** I know King David, and you're no David!

**Preacher:** WHA—HUH?

**God:** I said, "I AM WHO I AM."

**Preacher:** But…that's…that's what God used as an answer!

**God:** You're right, [name of preacher], it is.

**Preacher:** Do you mean to tell me that I'm supposed to believe that I'm sitting here and God is talking to me?

**God:** Does that surprise you?

**Preacher:** Well yes, it does! I mean, if I was in the sanctuary at church or something like that, I might believe it. But not in my living room.

**God:** Have I not promised that I'd be with you always?

**Preacher:** Well…yes…

**God:** Do you think that I keep my promises?

**Preacher:** Well yes, but…

**God:** Well?

**Preacher:** Well, I guess…I'm just surprised, that's all.

**God:** Why? You were just thanking me.

**Preacher:** What do you mean?

**God:** I just heard you say, "Thank God," and I decided to say, "You're welcome."

**Preacher:** That's just an expression; it doesn't mean anything.

**God:** Oh, so you really weren't thanking me?

**Preacher:** Wait a minute now. I didn't mean it that way. I mean, I really do appreciate everything you do for me and all, it's just that…

**God:** It's just what?

**Preacher:** It's just that this is my living room. I'm just taking a few minutes to relax…and you're the God of the grand and extraordinary, not the everyday!

**God:** That seems like a safe place to keep me.

**Preacher:** What do you mean?

**God:** It's safe—keeping me in the extraordinary, rather than letting me intrude into your everyday world.

**Preacher:** That's not what I meant! It just seems strange to think of you as here and now!

**God:** Where else do you think I would be?

**Preacher:** It just seems that I always think of you associated with the "big" projects.

**God:** Actually, I'm glad you mentioned "big" projects. I have a job for you!

**Preacher:** Whoa, wait a minute! This doesn't involve gopher wood, or boats, or sea journeys, or anything like that, does it? I mean, I can't swim and I get seasick, and I know you can find someone else who'd do a much better job than me…

**God:** [Name of preacher]…

**Preacher:** I mean, I appreciate the thought, but I've got a lot going on right now…

**God:** [Name of preacher]…

**Preacher:** And I'm not sure that I'd be all that good…

**God:** [Name of preacher]!!!

**Preacher:** Anyway. *(Pause.)* Be quiet, right?

**God:** Right! Better yet, "Be still, and know that I am God."

**Preacher:** Hey, I've heard that before!

**God:** Do you think you're the first one I've ever had this trouble with? I've heard all these excuses before! Jonah, Elijah, Moses—they all had excuses. Each one had all sorts of problems and reasons why he was the wrong person for the job, but he did it anyway! They could have given me a hundred excuses, but it finally came down to faith in my Word. You don't doubt that, do you?

**Preacher:** *(Wincing)* I suppose not. Well, what do you want?

**God:** That's better. Now, like I said, I have a job for you. I want you to do two things: I want you to "share" your faith and be a "steward" of your faith.

**Preacher:** That's all? No boats! No whales! That's it? I can do that, easy! I do that all the time, now!

**God:** Do you?

**Preacher:** Don't I? I mean, at least I think I do!?!

**God:** Explain to me what you think it means to share your faith.

**Preacher:** Well, that's easy. I tell people about what I believe, and then, I guess, I try to convince them to believe as well.

**God:** What do you mean, "convince"? I've asked you to be about the job of sharing.

**Preacher:** But isn't that part of the job?

**God:** You seem to have our jobs mixed up. It isn't part of your job description to convince anyone of anything. Your responsibility is to invite people to the faith—to let them know about it. Your job is to tell them what it means to you, and then to make it welcoming, or in one word: Share. Then it becomes their responsibility to decide whether or not they will allow their lives to be changed. You can't change their lives, and I won't. Only they can, by inviting me in!

**Preacher:** Is it really that simple? Just share?

**God:** Just share. And after you've shared, trust.

**Preacher:** What do you mean, "trust"?

**God:** For example, what do you mean when you say you want the church to be successful?

**Preacher:** Well, I suppose I mean that we're doing all the right things, our numbers are growing, our budget is growing, and we are gaining more influence in the community.

**God:** Why do you consider those the marks of success?

**Preacher:** Well, that's what it takes to be a success in our society.

**God:** So you believe success is dictated by society? So you're a societian, then? Someone who builds a life around the dictates and standards of society?

**Preacher:** Well no, at least I hope not. I think of myself as a Christian. I build my life around the teachings of Christ.

**God:** Then if you've shared and they've decided, you must trust me to do my part—to build new living creatures in Christ. That's what I do, and I'm good at it! All you have to do is share, and then it becomes their job to decide whether or not to allow me into their lives.

**Preacher:** But what about that second part, be a steward of the faith? I've got a feeling that you're going to tell me that I'm a bit weak in that one as well.

**God:** I'll let you decide for yourself. When you last preached a stewardship sermon, you told people that they could look into their checkbooks and learn about their values, right?

**Preacher:** Sure. I believe our hearts and hands go side by side. If we believe in something, like the work of the church, we support that belief with our gifts of talent and money. I live that, too! Don't tell me that I'm falling short there!

**God:** No. I'm quite aware that you've made tithing a priority in your life. And it doesn't seem to have hurt you.

**Preacher:** Not at all. In fact, we feel richer than ever. I do get frustrated with those people who say "Charity begins at home" for their explanation of why they don't sense an obligation to support the church. But I fail to see your point.

**God:** I understand your frustration, but we will save that discussion for another day. The point is that you've only mentioned one part of stewardship. There's another part you seem to have forgotten.

**Preacher:** Another part? What's that?

**God:** I have given you a most precious gift. It consists of 168 hours in every week. No one is richer or poorer in this gift. Everyone has the same amount. You can't give this resource away or misplace it; you can't buy any more for any amount of money; nor can you make more for yourself. The amount is fixed—you can only spend it, use it, or waste it. Now, just as in your stewardship sermon when you were talking about the stewardship of the dollar, there is a stewardship of time as well. Just like money, you can waste time, kill time, or lose time. How you choose to spend your time becomes an issue of stewardship as well.

**Preacher:** But don't I do enough? I'm always at the church until late, and, in fact, I'm headed back over there in just a few minutes. Are you asking me to spend more time there?

**God:** What I am asking you to do is to be a good steward of the time you have. Spend it wisely and in a meaningful manner. Attending meetings and doing the work of the church is important. An institution like the church wouldn't thrive without all the people who gather together to share their talents, personal gifts, and resources. But that's not what I'm talking about.

What I'm wondering is how wise a steward are you with the rest of your time? I'm not talking about the job time, but the rest of the time in your life. What do you do with it? Are you using it wisely?

**Preacher:** I guess I really don't know. I haven't really thought about it.

**God:** Well, it's about time you thought about it. How much quality time do you spend nurturing the children I have blessed you with? How much intentional time do you give to the person I have bonded with you as your spouse? How much time do you save for your own spiritual growth?

**Preacher:** It doesn't sound as if there's going to be much time left over!

**God:** That's the same excuse you used when you struggled against becoming a tither in the first place. You kept saying, "There won't be enough to go around." But what did you discover?

**Preacher:** *(Slowly, with a bit of wonder)* That there was plenty!

**God:** And what can you learn from that?

**Preacher:** Now that I think of it, I think I could do a better job of investing my time wisely. I've been wanting to do more fishing, and I'd love a good reason to get away from work more often and…

**God:** You're missing the point. Yes, you do need to take some time for yourself. That's OK, just like it's OK to occasionally spend money on yourself. But that's not the only way you need to spend your time. Just as in the stewardship of your finances, what have you learned?

**Preacher:** To place you first? Oh, I think I get it! I need to make you the first thing in my life! Take a portion of the time you've given me to use for prayer, meditation, worship, or Bible study. You know, that seems so simple!

**God:** It doesn't have to be complicated to be good.

**Preacher:** Just spend my "first time" with you, like a tithe…

**God:** That's the idea. Do you think you can handle it?

**Preacher:** I'm sure I can. Why, I probably waste more time than that during the day, sitting in traffic and killing time. Thanks, God. I think I needed this little talk.

**God:** I know.

**Preacher:** But I've got to go. I've got a church meeting…talk to you later.

**God:** I think I remember saying that I will be with you, always.

**Preacher:** You did, didn't you? I'll look forward to our next talk.

**God:** I'll be here…always.

# Assessing the Story

This particular dialogue was developed as a follow-up to a fall season of evangelism and stewardship. Both issues were addressed in the sermon, although in the typical Dialogue Sermon, it would be wiser to tackle one at a time. Developing the sermon around a single issue will help not only with the simplicity of delivery, but it allows the congregation to keep its focus.

Hopefully, as you read through "Excuse Me?" you noticed that the Dialogue Sermon provides the freedom to be straightforward with particular issues which, if spoken directly to the congregation, might otherwise cause defensive reactions. This freedom is one of the greatest strengths of the Dialogue Sermon.

# Other Creative Ideas for Dialogue Sermons

• The speaker could voice frustration with the institutional church and the tendency for it to change slowly. This could be contrasted with the church's ability to withstand popular fads and continue to spread the gospel even as civilizations and cultures rise and fall.

• The speaker could respond to a horror or disaster in the daily newspaper. How could a loving God allow this to happen? This dialogue might center on the loving Spirit of God that supports us even in the face of the evil of the world. This might take the form of a contrast between the human image of a God that "makes" bad things happen and the God that loves and nurtures us "when" bad things happen.

• The speaker could engage in dialogue about the differences between the "church" (the local congregation) and the Church (the universal body of Christ). How is it possible to be one body and yet so different? How can others claim to be Christians yet hold different beliefs?

• If the Dialogue Sermon is used at the beginning of a meeting, it could take the form of whatever the particular agenda is. For example, if the worship committee is going to discuss a change in worship, the dialogue might explore the reasons we worship in the first place.

• For use at the beginning of a board meeting in which members will be discussing the appointment or election of new leaders, the dialogue might focus on the differences between the human standard for leadership versus that of God's.

PASTOR LUPNER DIDN'T NOTICE UNTIL HE WAS HALFWAY INTO HIS SERMON THAT HE HAD MISTAKENLY BROUGHT HIS SEVEN-YEAR-OLD'S BOOK REPORT RATHER THAN HIS SERMON.

# CHAPTER 4

# The Duet Sermon

# TELLING THE STORY

I n music the term "duet" refers to two people or two musical instruments blending their unique, individual sounds to create a music quality beyond the abilities of the individual performers. For similar instruments (a violin duet) or dissimilar instruments (the jazz piano and the bass), it is the blending of the skills and the abilities that each performer brings to the performance that creates the distinctive sound of the duet.

Just as there is room for the duet in music, so there is in the communication of the gospel. The Duet Sermon may take many forms, from the rich heritage of the Jewish Haggadah and its stylized questions and answers[4] to the reading of Scripture and interpretation used by some congregations to celebrate the beginning of Advent with the Hanging of the Greens.

> *As its name implies, the Duet Sermon is presented by two readers. One reader begins with a question, passage, or poem; and the second reader responds with a related or contrasting piece.*

As its name implies, the Duet Sermon is presented by two readers. One reader begins with a question, passage, or poem; and the second reader responds with a related or contrasting piece. It's not necessary for the materials to have been written together or even to be completely complementary for the duet to work. Actually, the selection of materials that are somewhat different in either content or time period can be quite effective in bringing new light to familiar stories.

As you begin to prepare the Duet Sermon, first ask, What is its purpose and what do I want to communicate? It's very important to decide in the beginning what the purpose is because without an established objective it's easy to lose focus when choosing the readings for the duet.

Next decide how the voices of two individuals can be blended to create a unique reading, a reading that cannot be achieved by a single voice. As the speakers interact with each other through the reading, your goal, hopefully, will be achieved. Traditional reader interaction isn't the only way to create a Duet Sermon. Two speakers who appear as though they aren't aware of each other can present a very powerful sermon by using contrasting material. In the sample sermon (p. 65), the "diary" of Job is juxtaposed on the "diary" of a Holocaust survivor. By integrating stories from different times and places, readers with no apparent interaction can provide new understanding of ancient ideas.

Another example of contrasting stories woven together to create a powerful message might be the sharing of the life stories of two women, one ancient and one modern. The first reader might, for example, tell of her shame at living a life of adultery. Perhaps she does this out of sinful lust. Perhaps she sells herself to buy food for her abandoned children. Subsequently, the woman is caught and brought before Jesus, both to receive punishment and to test the man Jesus. You'll recognize this familiar story based on the text from John 8:1-11. This ancient Bible passage makes for an excellent contrast to a story about a modern woman who also for unknown reasons works the city streets as a prostitute. Weary beyond exhaustion, old beyond her years, and seeking hope to rebuild her life, she turns to a church for help. The women's stories might converge or separate depending on the conclusion. The modern woman can either be received with forgiveness and affirmation or can be greeted suspiciously and quickly referred to the appropriate agency.

> *When developing a Duet Sermon, it isn't necessary to draw conclusions or make pithy moral statements. An effective duet will "hook" the congregation and then present a dilemma that the congregation must solve on its own.*

When developing a Duet Sermon, it isn't necessary to draw conclusions or make pithy moral statements. An effective duet will "hook" the congregation and then present a dilemma that the congregation must solve on its own.

# CHOOSING THE MATERIAL

So the preacher can choose material that is directly related or material that is dissimilar or unrelated.

The biblical account from Luke 10 offers an excellent example of related material. It's not difficult to imagine the duet that would take place between the thoughts of Mary and the thoughts of Martha. Another way to use related material is by juxtapositioning Scripture and the interpretation of Scripture. This combination can be especially powerful as a means of relating various stories of our faith. Used during Advent, the collection of prophecy and the stories of prophetic fulfillment can make for a powerful telling of the Christ story. In a similar manner, the duet might blend readings from the Old and New Testaments focusing on a single topic such as God's love.

When putting together a duet using dissimilar material, the two stories should have sufficient common ground so the relationship between them will be revealed as the sermon develops. In other words, two seemingly unrelated materials are presented in a manner that challenges listeners to determine their commonalties and then make personal faith decisions for their lives.

Let me repeat: Care should be given to not over-explain the link between the readings. It's important to give God's grace room to communicate beyond the words of the readers. Too many explanations can actually hinder a broader understanding and constrict the message.

Consider presenting the autobiographical story of a modern teenager who is expecting her first child. Single and pregnant, facing a disapproving family and a doubting father-to-be, she relates her tale of rejection and subsequent acceptance. The reflections of a teenage Mary awaiting the birth of Jesus would serve as an exceptional piece to complete this duet. The similarities and contrasts of the two stories will stand by themselves. They need no explanation. Familiarity with the biblical account of Mary's story, along with subtle similarities, will serve as the hook to pull the congregation into the message in a very powerful way. Through this particular duet, it becomes possible to present a lucid view of Mary's experiences during the months preceding Christ's birth. The impact should be tremendous as listeners gain a deeper understanding of the biblical account as well as a new vision for ministry in the church and community.

*Each specific reading will have particular strengths that recommend it for certain methods of presentation. For example, the positioning of speakers can suggest something about their importance and can even convey certain sympathies before the sermon begins.*

# SETTING THE SCENE

The visual setting of the duet may take any of several forms. Each specific reading will have particular strengths that recommend it for certain methods of presentation. For example, the positioning of speakers can suggest something about their importance and can even convey certain sympathies before the sermon begins.

A dialogue between Mary and Martha might take place on equal ground such as the middle of the worship platform or from two podiums in the front of the church. The "sinful woman" from Luke 7:36-50, on the other hand, might stand "below" a proper woman. In this case, one reader standing below the other will immediately establish an interesting visual relationship between the two. In one way, the reader standing closer to the congregation has a greater opportunity to appeal to its sympathies. As a general rule of thumb, a "sacred" speaker should speak from a raised platform area, and a "secular" speaker from the floor of the sanctuary. Like any rule, this one can be broken depending on the visual effect the preacher is trying to achieve. Imagine this scene: The "proper" woman stands on the worship platform confronting the "sinful" woman on the floor. As the duet develops, the women gradually change places. This scene would be a very powerful illustration of Christ's forgiveness for the sinful woman and condemnation of the proper woman for her lack of forgiveness. The kinesthetic learners will feel it, the visual learners will see it, the auditory learners will hear it, and everyone will understand it!

> *The kinesthetic learners will feel it, the visual learners will see it, the auditory learners will hear it, and everyone will understand it!*

There is much to recommend keeping Bible stories on the raised platform. The area from which God's Word is typically spoken provides a very powerful symbol. Moving secular accounts away from the pulpit provides freedom to emphasize differences in source and content. When considering a setting for the Duet Sermon, you will want to make logistical decisions based on your material, the space in which you have to work, and the message you seek to convey. Don't overlook this simple but important step. And remember, even the best visual presentation will fail if listeners cannot hear and understand what is being said!

# DELIVERY

While memorization of the material is wonderful, it's not always practical, and there are several good alternatives. One possibility is to deliver the material in a "reader's theater" format, where the readers use music stands or podiums to hold their scripts. If you use this format, it's advisable to make copies of the script so the readers won't have to turn pages while reading. The material should be sufficiently familiar to them so that the script exists only for reference.

*During the presentation, the speakers should look up from the podium or pulpit to speak and then bow their heads when they are silent. This will not only provide visual clues as to "where the action is," but will also draw attention to a particular speaker even during prolonged pauses. (The pauses can be as eloquent as words.)*

During the presentation, the speakers should look up from the podium or pulpit to speak and then bow their heads when they are silent. This will not only provide visual clues as to "where the action is," but will also draw attention to a particular speaker even during prolonged pauses. (The pauses can be as eloquent as words.)

Another presentation style is the duet interpretation taught in many speech classes. Simple notebooks, containing the script and held by the readers, will allow for easy mobility in the presentation area. As in the reader's theater format, scripts should be copied and arranged to eliminate page turns as each reader presents his or her material. In addition, eye contact should only be made by the speaker currently presenting. The nonspeaking reader should look at the script and in a sense "disappear." Whatever method is used, success will depend a great deal on the readers' familiarity with the script

*As in all creative sermon presentations, the more time the presenters have spent practicing, the more natural it will sound to the listeners. Besides, practice provides a very effective method to "proofread" the material.*

As in all creative sermon presentations, the more time the presenters have spent practicing, the more natural it will sound to the listeners. Besides, practice provides a very effective method to "proofread" the material. To practice the Duet Sermon, have the readers begin by reading the script aloud. As they read, they can work together to determine timing, style, and volume of the presentation. During practice, questions can be addressed, such as Who should speak loudly and when? Who should speak softly and when? Should there be pauses between the readers' parts? Are there particular lines in which the words should almost overlap?

# Sample Duet Sermon

## Introduction

"Where Is God?" was originally developed for Holocaust Sunday.[5] It is a Duet Sermon based on the book of Job and Elie Wiesel's *Night*.[6]

In the original presentation, the first reader, presenting the material from Job, stood on the worship platform and was a man. The second reader, presenting adaptations of Wiesel's *Night,* stood to the side on the floor below and was a woman. The material was presented in a reader's theater format, using the pulpit for the first reader and a music stand for the second reader. Both readers had microphones so that every word, shouted or whispered, would be heard clearly. No costumes or actions were used; however, a range of vocal inflections was incorporated to convey the emotions of the authors.

# WHERE IS GOD?

**Reader 1:** (*Conversationally*) In the land of Uz there lived a man whose name was Job. This man was blameless and upright; he feared God and shunned evil.

**Reader 2:** (*Conversationally*) The enforcer at the camp was called the Oberkapo. He was a tall man and had hundreds of prisoners who worked under him. He was well loved by them because he'd never uttered a mean word and never lifted a hand to any of them. His young helper was called a pipel. He seemed always to have a sad face, but like the Oberkapo, was also well loved by everyone.

**Reader 1:** One day the angels came to present themselves before the Lord, and Satan also came with them. The Lord said to Satan, "Where have you come from?" Satan answered the Lord, "From roaming through the earth and going back and forth in it." Then the Lord said to Satan, "Have you considered my servant Job? There is no one on earth like him; he is blameless and upright, a man who fears God and shuns evil." Does Job fear God for nothing?" Satan replied. "Have you not put a hedge around him and his household and everything he has? You have blessed the work of his hands, so that his flocks and herds are spread throughout the land. But stretch out your hand and strike everything he has, and he will surely curse you to your face." The Lord said to Satan, "Very well, then, everything he has is in your hands.

**Reader 2:** One day there was an explosion. Sabotage was suspected and the Gestapo investigated. The Oberkapo was arrested and tortured, but they couldn't get anything out of him.

**Reader 1:** One day when Job's sons and daughters were feasting and drinking wine at the oldest brother's house, messengers came to Job and told him that his servants and all of his livestock had been killed. Yet another messenger came and said, "Your sons and daughters were feasting and drinking wine at the oldest brother's house, when suddenly a mighty wind swept in from the desert and struck the four corners of the house. It collapsed on them and they are dead, and I am the only one who has escaped to tell you!" At this, Job got up and tore his robe and shaved his head. Then he fell to the ground in worship and said: (*Loudly and in anguish*) "Naked I came from my mother's womb, and naked I will depart. The Lord gave and the Lord has taken away; may the name of the Lord be praised."

**Reader 2:** (*Quietly, with horror*) Since the Oberkapo wouldn't provide any names, he was transferred to Auschwitz and never heard from again.

**Reader 1:** On another day the angels came to present themselves before the Lord, and Satan also came with them to present himself before him. And the Lord said to Satan, "Where have you come from? Satan answered the Lord, "From roaming through the earth and going back and forth in it." Then the Lord said to Satan, "Have you considered my servant Job? There is no one on earth like him; he is blameless and upright, a man who fears God and shuns evil."

**Reader 2:** (*Quietly*) The sad-faced little helper was left behind. Because of his friendship with the Oberkapo, he was arrested and tortured. He too would not speak a word.

**Reader 1:** "Skin for skin! Satan replied. "A man will give all he has for his own life. But stretch out your hand and strike his flesh and bones, and he will surely curse you to your face." The Lord said to Satan, "Very well, then, he is in your hands."

**Reader 2:** *(With disgust)* While God agreed to allow Satan to inflict Job with loathsome sores from the soles of his feet to the crown of his head, the Lord commanded that the life of Job be spared. The Gestapo received no such instructions. *(Pause.)* The SS sentenced the little sad-faced angel to death. One day when we came back from work, we saw three gallows raised up. Roll call. SS all around, machine guns pointed at us; the traditional ceremony of death. Three victims in chains. *(Quietly)* One of them was the little servant, the sad-eyed angel.

**Reader 1:** His wife said to him, "Are you still holding on to your integrity? Curse God and die!" He replied, "You are talking like a foolish woman. Shall we accept good from God, and not trouble?" In all this, Job did not sin in what he said.

**Reader 2:** To hang a young boy in front of so many spectators was no small matter, and the SS seemed preoccupied.

**Reader 1:** When Job's three best friends heard about all the troubles that had come upon him, they came to be with him and comfort him. But when they saw him from a distance, they could hardly recognize him. They began to weep aloud. Then they sat on the ground with him for seven days and seven nights. No one said a word to him, because they saw how great his suffering was.

**Reader 2:** Everyone was watching, but even in the shadow of the gallows, the pipel was showing no sign of strain.

**Reader 1:** After this, Job opened his mouth and cursed the day of his birth. *(Loudly, with misery)* "May the day of my birth perish. Why did I not perish at birth, and die as I came from the womb? Why is light given to those in misery? What I feared has come upon me; what I dreaded has happened to me."

**Reader 2:** But the executioner wouldn't carry out his duties and was replaced by three members of the SS.

**Reader 1:** The three friends of Job answered Job's anguished questions by saying, "You have instructed many. You have strengthened the weak in the face of evil. But now it has come to you and you are impatient. Consider now: 'Who, being innocent, has ever perished?' As I have observed, those who plow evil and those who sow trouble reap it."

**Reader 2:** Two other victims mounted the gallows with the young boy.

**Reader 1:** "For hardship does not spring from the soil," shouted one of Job's friends, "nor does trouble simply sprout from the ground."

**Reader 2:** Nooses were placed around each of their necks.

**Reader 1:** "If it were I, I would appeal to God. I would lay my cause before him. He thwarts the plans of the crafty…so that the poor have hope, and injustice shuts its mouth."

**Reader 2:** *(Loudly)* Someone shouted, "Long live liberty."

**Reader 1:** "From six calamities he will rescue you; in seven no harm will befall you."

**Reader 2:** *(Very quietly)* The child was silent.

**Reader 1:** *(Slowly and with great weariness of spirit)* Job replied, "I have heard many things like these; miserable comforters are you all. I also could speak like you, if you were in my place; Surely, O God, you have worn me out."

**Reader 2:** *(Whispering)* The child was silent.

**Reader 1:** *(Continuing from before)* "Men have gaped at me with their mouths. God has given me up to the ungodly and cast me into the hands of the wicked. How often is it that the lamp of the wicked is put out? How then will you comfort me with empty nothings? There is nothing left of your answers but falsehood."

**Reader 2:** *(With more power)* Someone behind me asked, "Where is God? But everyone else was silently weeping. As we marched past the gallows, two of the ropes were still, but the third was moving. The child was still alive.

**Reader 1:** *(With strength)* Then Job answered, "Why are not times of judgment kept by the Almighty, and why do those who know him never see his ways? From out of the city the dying groan, and the soul of the wounded cries for help…

**Reader 2:** He hung there somewhere between life and death for more than half an hour.

**Reader 1:** *(Finishing the sentence)* "…yet God pays no attention to their prayer."

**Reader 2:** *(With horror)* As I passed in front of him, I could tell that he was still alive.

**Reader 1:** And Elihu said, "Do you think this is just? I would like to reply to you. Look up at the heavens and see; gaze at the clouds so high above you. Men cry out under a load of oppressions, but no one says, "Where is God?"

**Reader 2:** *(Echoing the last sentence of Reader 1)* Again, the man behind me asked, "Where is God?"

**Reader 1:** Then the Lord answered Job out of the storm, "Who is this that darkens my counsel without knowledge? Where were you when I laid the earth's foundations? Does the hawk take flight by your wisdom and spread his wings toward the south? Does the eagle soar at your command and build his nest on high? Will the one who contends with the Almighty correct him? Let him who accuses God, answer him!"

**Reader 2:** Where is he? A voice within me answered, "Here…he is hanging here on this gallows…"

**Reader 1:** *(Pause.)* Then Job replied to the Lord: "I know that you can do all things. Surely I spoke of things I did not understand, things too wonderful for me to know. Now my eyes have seen you. Therefore I despise myself and repent in dust and ashes."

# Assessing the Story

The telling of these two stories of suffering makes for a haunting and moving experience of two men searching desperately to find and understand God. "Where Is God?" provides an example of just how powerful a sermon of this type can be. Sometimes suffering can be so overwhelming that it's almost beyond human comprehension. When this happens, it becomes easy to intellectualize the event. However, as this Duet Sermon illustrates, playing two stories off of one another personalizes the message in a way that can make it very real to the listeners.

# Other Creative Ideas for Duet Sermons

The possibilities for developing powerful Duet Sermons are almost endless. Check out the following ideas.

• Contrast contemporary accounts of wealth. Gather newspaper or magazine articles about get-rich-quick schemes or enticements to spend money on luxury items. Contrast the articles with readings from the Old Testament, such as Psalm 49 (the folly of trusting in riches). A Duet Sermon such as this could also be used as an introduction to the parable about the rich man in Luke 12:13-21.

• Compare a contemporary account of an individual whose life is in turmoil and without direction with the words of Psalm 22 detailing David's belief that God would lead him out of despair. As an additional creative element, invite a third reader to read from the contemporary poem "Footprints," by Margaret Fishback Powers.

• Although it took time and energy, a humorous and well-received version of the duet involved one reader quoting contemporary bumper stickers (bumper sticker theology!) and the other reader reading Scripture verses appropriate to each issue.

• A powerful contrasting duet from nonbiblical sources blended a mixture of cold war rhetoric with *The War Prayer*, by Mark Twain. This work focuses on the power of prayer as well as recognizing what the words of prayer can mean to the "enemy." Combining materials from these two sources form a stunning reflection on the issue of praying for God's intervention.

PASTOR WAYNE KLEMPER DIDN'T RESPOND WELL TO CRITICISM.

# CHAPTER 5

# The Letter From Home

# TELLING THE STORY

Nothing is quite as familiar or as comfortable as a letter from home. It can remind us of old friends with all of their familiar follies and foibles and of places that never really seem to change, at least in our memories. A letter from home is an opportunity to step outside the limits of everyday life and into the timelessness of memory. "Home" is a peculiar place where both fact and fiction reside—a place that is a mixture of the familiar and the strange, the commonplace and the truly extraordinary.

Radio entertainer Garrison Keillor has spurred this form of communication to new heights. He created an imaginary hometown in a location known as Lake Woebegon. This wonderfully familiar town, with its well-known residents and well-known businesses, has found its way into the hearts of a generation of radio fans.[7] The most interesting part about Garrison Keillor's Lake Woebegon stories is that to get something from them it's not necessary to know personally any of the people he talks about. That's because when we hear about the residents, we discover we really do "know them." They are the people from our own life experiences, from our churches, and from our communities. The names and details may be different, but we know them, nonetheless.

*The strength of the Letter From Home is based upon the simple fact that there are certain stereotypical people who come from anyone's hometown. Sometimes the stereotypes run true, sometimes they don't, but they usually sound familiar.*

The strength of the Letter From Home is based upon the simple fact that there are certain stereotypical people who could come from anyone's hometown. Sometimes the stereotypes run true, sometimes they don't, but they usually sound familiar. Sometimes they may even be discordant enough to jar us with unfamiliarity. Yet through it all, the Letter From Home is always a close, personal, and intimate picture of a life we either remember or recognize. The Letter From Home has the ability to make us both comfortable and nostalgic and then turn our comfort zone into a tool that teaches a lesson.

*The Letter From Home has the ability to make us both comfortable and nostalgic and then turn our comfort zone into a tool that teaches a lesson.*

Although Paul the apostle typically wrote letters to specific churches and addressed specific situations many centuries ago, we can still learn from his writings today. As we read Paul's letters it is as though he was writing to us. Although the locations and names of the people have changed, most of the issues and problems are recognizable in our lives today. The issues of Paul's day are really the issues of today. Actually, most of today's problems aren't all that unique; they are the same problems that have been a part of the human condition throughout history.

In a similar manner, a sermon presented in the form of a Letter From Home, whether imaginary like Garrison Keillor's or real, can speak to issues common in the lives of a contemporary congregation. The real beauty of this type of sermon is that it allows listeners to lay aside defensiveness such as rationalization and justification and hear something in a way they have never heard before. At the very least, it allows the preacher the liberty to speak to a variety of issues in a less threatening or confrontational manner.

After delivering a sermon in the form of a Letter From Home, I have yet to have a listener suggest that I was preaching at their problem. On the other hand, I have frequently heard comments such as "they sound just like us!" (That's the point!)

*The real beauty of this type of sermon is that it allows listeners to lay aside defensiveness such as rationalization and justification and hear something in a way they have never heard before.*

The key to turning a Letter From Home into an effective sermon is in blending the commonplace with the extraordinary. In other words, it is using the events of everyday life to point beyond the character and toward the extraordinary intervention of God. The challenge in creating a sermon like this comes in taking a specific event and trying to frame it so it has both a universal and personal application.

A sermon with a universal application assures listeners that the preacher isn't preaching "at them." The message itself is tied together by a lesson or theme that applies to all people and is obvious to the listener that it does so. This doesn't imply that a preacher cannot or should not be direct in a message. But if listeners feel the preacher is getting too personal or coming a little too close for comfort, they will use their built-in defense mechanisms to build a wall between themselves and the message. Once the wall is built, it goes without saying, the listeners will get very little, if anything, from the message. For this reason, the Letter From Home can create the perfect conditions for addressing issues unhindered by listeners' defensiveness, prejudice, and other barriers commonly used for self protection.

On the other hand, the Letter From Home has an enticing personal element as well. It actually speaks to listeners in a very personal and private manner, slipping behind their natural defenses. As I mentioned at the beginning of this chapter, this comes as a result of listener's nostalgic recognition of common people, places, and events. A sermon presented in this manner allows people to look into the lives of others and see themselves and God more clearly.

*After delivering a sermon in the form of a Letter From Home, I have yet to have a listener suggest that I was preaching at their problem. On the other hand, I have frequently heard comments such as "they sound just like us!" (That's the point!)*

# CHOOSING AND DEVELOPING THE STORY LINE

Every Letter From Home needs a place of origin. Determining the location of the town will set the stage to create this type of sermon. One place to begin might be your own hometown. Using your hometown has certain advantages including your own personal wealth of experiences and familiarity with the details of the setting. The disadvantages, however, may outweigh the advantages.

There are ethical considerations that come with preaching about real people and their problems. Revealing the details about a person's intimate life brings up questions about breaches in confidentiality. Whatever setting you choose, it should be obscure enough to allow no connections between hometown characters and actual people, living or dead. If it appears that I'm being overly sensitive about this subject, it's simply because the Letter From Home provides a very tempting context in which to publicly display real people and their problems without intending any harm. It is difficult to imagine the feelings of congregation members who think there is an outside chance that their weaknesses will to be used as object lessons for others. The point is to keep the characters and events imaginary, if for no other reason than simple courtesy and compassion. The focus should be on the letter, as it is presented, and not on trying to guess who the preacher's talking about! A preacher should never be the instrument of public invasion into the lives of others, no matter how unintentional.

*There are ethical considerations that come with preaching about real people and their problems. Revealing the details about a person's intimate life brings up questions about breaches in confidentiality.*

An imaginary hometown populated by imaginary people with real problems will undoubtedly provide the most fruitful context in which to build your sermon.

As you make decisions about a hometown, consider if it will be rural or urban? a large city or a small town? northern or southern? coastal or foreign? What are the people like? Are they sophisticated or simple? talented or commonplace? What "characters" populate the town?

As you answer these questions, draw from your knowledge of people you have met and have had experiences with. The easiest people to introduce to your audience are stereotypes, painted with a compassionate brush. It's important to use people your audience will identify with. The characters should be three-dimensional people whose lives are similar to your listeners.

The purpose in presenting a verbal portrait of a character is not to be judgmental, but rather to allow the listeners to see their own reflection in the eyes of the character. Hometown character development is a case of "less being more." It is not necessary to explain every action or every character trait. Trust your listeners to move to their own conclusions resulting from your skillfully painted verbal portrait.

Ideas for hometown characters can come in many different ways. Regularly watching televised news channels and reading local newspapers can provide ideas for development of characters. Small town newspapers often publish local society columns that spark ideas for wonderful nostalgic characters, both humorous and touching.

*Ideas for hometown characters can come in many different ways. Regularly watching televised news channels and reading local newspapers can provide ideas for development of characters. Small town newspapers often publish local society columns that spark ideas for wonderful nostalgic characters, both humorous and touching.*

For purposes of illustration, let me tell you about my own hometown. The town is East Hollister located in the heart of Ozark country. It's a small "hill" town populated by a variety of folks who are surprising in both their diversity and their industry (or lack thereof). Yup! There are such folk as hillbillies in East Hollister! Their claim-to-fame, if you could call it that, is their commitment to stay isolated from the rest of the world. An outsider will find a proper, yet cool welcome in East Hollister. Even the residents that have moved into town, say twenty-five years ago, are still considered "new folk."

Even though East Hollister isn't considered a "tiny town" in the overall geographic picture of things, there's no need for locals to use turn signals when driving because everyone knows where they're going anyway.

It's also not unheard of to have some town folk belong to more than one local congregation, such as both the Catholic and Christian churches (just in case!).

The town itself doesn't change much; a new building or the loss of an old one is definitely big news. The local newspaper, delivered twice weekly, prints a society column. In it are included notices of who went where for dinner parties, who is traveling, who is visiting family, and who is being visited by family. The events of the 4-H or FFA are more likely to make the front page than the national news. A hard-hitting editorial series would never be stopped as the result of outside pressure. However, it might be axed immediately, following a reproving phone call from the mother of the editor-in-chief.

The local schools are academically solid and staffed by teachers who have taught multiple generations. Of course, the most important qualification possessed by a teacher in East Hollister is the experience of teaching multiple generations.

The people of East Hollister don't consider themselves hicks; they're just selective in their interaction with the world. Some families have long-standing feuds. Of course that can get especially complicated if kids from two feuding families decide to date.

*It is not necessary to explain every action or every character trait. Trust your listeners to move to their own conclusions resulting from your skillfully painted verbal portrait.*

East Hollister is definitely rich in its character and populated by a variety of people who can provide a wealth of illustrations. (And, if you're interested, I'm actually from a large suburb of Kansas City but with ties through my grandmother to the Ozarks. But the illustration shows how simple it is to create an imaginary hometown that can effectively become the foundation for a humorous yet meaningful sermon.)

Once the hometown has been created, and its population has been identified, the next step is to determine what stories the characters will share. These are stories gleaned from the news, the preacher's own life experiences, and stories of the Bible updated to relate to the people of today. A bit of hometown nostalgia sprinkled on top of the truths of Scripture will bring the sermon to life.

# SETTING THE SCENE

I t's important that the Letter From Home be delivered from somewhere other than the traditional speaking platform or pulpit. The letter is unabashedly a combination of the real and the imaginary and definitely takes artistic license to illustrate certain points. A move from the sacred platform where the Word of God is typically presented will help keep it that way. Tongue-in-cheek humor and the exaggerated style used in a Letter From Home will be more acceptable if presented in a neutral location. Additionally, visual and kinesthetic learners will appreciate the preacher's moving from the normal speaking area to a chair. A small table and a letter in an envelope will complete the setting.

*A bit of hometown nostalgia sprinkled on top of the truths of Scripture will bring the sermon to life.*

# DELIVERY

The Letter From Home is most effective when it is simple, straightforward, and able to make fun of itself. Probably the most compelling place to deliver a sermon of this type is from a comfortable chair located at the center of the chancel or platform. Just before reading, take a moment to get comfortable. Take off your coat, kick off your shoes, loosen your tie; act as though you're at home. Home is usually the best place to relax and read a letter like this.

*As you read, occasionally take a moment to look up and explain certain details. This will draw the listeners into the drama as though they play a part in the letter.*

As you read, occasionally take a moment to look up and explain certain details. This will draw the listeners into the drama as though they play a part in the letter. It also allows you to explain particular details, make comments about the characters or setting, and otherwise share information that would normally not be a part of the letter.

# Sample Letter From Home

## Introduction

The following sermon example, "Widow's Mite," is based on Mark 12:38-44. It was delivered as part of a congregational focus on stewardship.[8]

# WIDOW'S MITE

*(The first section of the sermon is addressed to the congregation as the preacher gets comfortable.)*

Friends, it's been a long time since I shared with you a letter from my hometown. But the post office managed to find me recently, and I thought you might enjoy hearing about some of the happenings back home in the East Hollister Church.

Now, some of you will remember I've shared a few stories from that church before—my home church. It's a place like most other home churches—muddling through some of the same old issues and made up of some of the same wonderful people, with a few colorful characters and one or two certifiable nut cases thrown in—my family excluded, of course. Anyway, here's the letter.

*(Open the envelope and begin to "read" the letter.)*

Dear Skip,

*(Looking up to explain)*

That's what they call me to keep me separate from my father who's also a Murray. It used to get pretty confusing in my high school days, especially when someone called and asked for "Big Murray" or "Little Murray." Mom never knew who to call to the phone. So my closest friends always knew me as Skip.

*(Reading again)*

I thought I'd take a few minutes and catch you up on what's happening around here in East Hollister. I started thinking about this when we were talking about your stewardship campaign on the phone the other day. I know you tell me that preaching's "your" job, so I thought I'd write you about Mrs. Adele. You remember her; she was old even when you were a kid.

Maybe you'll remember that Adele's husband was named Red. The only time I ever saw her lose control was when her Red died. Red was her entire life. Forty years they had been husband and wife. They had raised three children together—good children, successful children. In fact, the children were so successful that they moved away from this tiny town where their parents had raised them.

Each Sunday, of course, they phone. Occasionally, one of the grandkids would get hold of the phone and tell Adele the latest joke making rounds in the school yard…like, What kind of teeth can you buy for a dollar? Buck teeth.

*(Looking up)*

She loves those silly jokes.

*(Reading again)*

And at Christmas each of them tries to make it back here to East Hollister, at least every other year. Of course, they have responsibilities to their spouses' families too. Adele longed to see them more often, but she understands. She knows they do the best they can.

Well anyway, Red was a fine man, but he didn't leave much behind for Adele to live on. The little bit of insurance he did leave didn't go very far. I was so glad her house was paid for. I don't know what she would have done otherwise. I know her children make fun of her frugal ways—how she turns down the heat and wears extra clothing in the winter. Red used to say she could pinch a penny so hard, it cried uncle!

Adele's money doesn't go very far nowadays. And I know how much she loves being able to buy her grandkids a gift from time to time. I also know that she loves her church. Adele once told me, not in pride mind you, but during a time of sharing at a women's circle meeting, that she and Red always tithed. That didn't surprise me. I know them, and I'd be willing to bet that they stayed on that mark even when they couldn't afford it."We give first to the Lord," Red would say, and they always did. Adele still keeps up that tradition, even though it's been quite a few years since Red died.

Now you need to understand that part of my letter is about that new young pastor we've got. Oh, I really like him, but he has managed to get things pretty stirred up around here. "There's not enough room in this old building," he says. Of course, he's right. A lot of the space we have at church really isn't fit for much of anything. He says it's all about putting together a program for young people, and for families with young children. He believes we need to keep them active and busy so that they won't get into trouble. I've heard you say a lot of the same things. You two would probably get along well enough.

Well, we didn't have much of what he calls programming when I was growing up, and I never did seem to get into trouble! We stayed active and busy enough! It took the whole family to keep a household running then. But times have changed and we have to change with them, I suppose. I remember you preaching once that the "message is eternal, but the method changes constantly." I suppose you're right.

Now Bea Jimson doesn't like our pastor at all. She says he caters too much to everyone else. Of course, it's not in Bea's nature to like a preacher. I doubt that Jesus would have been hired if she were on the search committee. I'm sure he would have disappointed her somehow. The apostle Paul would have definitely given her fits. I overheard her tell the new preacher the other day, "If God were still alive he'd be shocked at some of the changes you're making!" (I thought that the preacher did an admirable job of not laughing!) So you'd be right in suspecting she's not a big supporter of new programs, and definitely wants nothing to do with the idea of a building fund. I can't remember her exact words, but "Over my dead body!" was in there somewhere.

Adele says, "Bea's wrong about the pastor. He really cares for us older folks. I can understand that he is more comfortable with some of the younger ones. He's closer to their age. And besides that, after listening to Bea, it wouldn't surprise me if he did want to stay away from us. But we're not like Bea, and I think he knows that."

Well, I'm definitely excited about some of the new people who are coming to our church. Every time we get visitors, I tell them about the new life in our church. I tell them about our choir and the new families that are joining.

To tell the truth, I don't see anything wrong with a new building. Some of my happiest memories as a girl are from church hayrides, roasting S'mores, and playing games in the church basement. I don't see anything wrong with a good place for people to gather, a good place to learn, and a safe place for the youngsters to play.

Now Adele's a different story. I know a good part of what was troubling her about this whole program. You can tell by the way she lives that she knows the importance of making the church a part of her everyday life. So I can understand her dilemma.

The other evening she caught me after choir practice and asked, "Why did they put me in this position? I already tithe. Now they've added this building program and they're asking people to make a three-year pledge. Why, I may not even be around in three years. It's not fair. Besides they're asking people to come forward and leave pledge cards at the front. I don't really like parading my giving in front of everybody. Like Red always said, 'The peacock doesn't give half as much as the hen, it just makes a better show of it.' I'll bet some of those who are making big gifts don't even tithe. I definitely want to do my part, but I can only give a little bit."

When I called Adele this morning, she told me she prayed about it last night. She said, "I reminded the Lord that I already tithed. I told him that I didn't have a whole lot left over. I asked him if a couple dollars a week would be sufficient. He didn't say anything so I offered three dollars. That's more than a 150 dollars a year and more than 450 in three years. They need a thousand times that much. I hate to feel like I'm letting them down, but it's the best I can do."

Well Skip, that's what she decided to do. But there's no way she was going "down front" to do it. She decided to hand her card to Don, the usher. He said he'd make sure the card was turned in.

Now Skip, I'm sure you'll appreciate this part. On Sunday, Pastor Ed tried not to notice who was bringing their pledge cards to the front and who wasn't. Most of the people in the church supported the drive and came forward. Most of the young families, of course, were excited.

Last Sunday we invited the pastor over for dinner. He confessed that it bothered him that the overall giving level of the church was so low. He said people thought nothing of buying a new car or a camper, but the amount they gave to the church was a pittance. Actually, he thought it was funny. "The Bible talks about a narrow road to heaven," he said. "But so many families are buying luxurious RVs and going on fancy vacations. If there really is a narrow road to heaven, half of them would get stuck and have to walk." But then you could tell he felt ashamed of himself.

I've heard you talk sometimes, Skip, about what it would be like if everyone in the church gave their fair share of time and financial support. You said there would be no need for drives like this one. There would be plenty of funds for the church to work in a way it's never worked before. But this is the real world, and there are many people in the church who are really doing the very best they can.

Last Sunday I saw Pastor Ed looking out over the congregation. He already knew that Bea would not budge from her pew when the pledges were collected. I suspect he never will figure Bea out. She's one of the most faithful members of the church, but also one of the most negative. I know he doesn't want to drive Bea away. He even told me that. Pastor Ed just wants her to have a positive spirit. I wonder what he'd do if Bea walked into church one morning with a smile on her face, spreading words of encouragement to everyone. Pastor Ed once said that he'd always wanted to see pigs fly. Oh well, nobody promised him the ministry would be easy.

I continued to watched him on pledge Sunday. His eye wandered over to Adele. You could just see his heart sink. I think he really had been counting on Adele. He knew she wouldn't be able to give much and even wondered how she survived on the little bit of income she had. But still, he needed her support. Adele is one of those souls who will never say a mean thing about anyone. Pastor Ed knew that of all the senior members in the church, she was his strongest supporter. Could it be that she was opposed to the programs and new building? Could it be that all the hard work had been in vain? You could just see it all in his eyes.

If the church didn't raise the entire amount in pledges today, the Board had already decided they would put off the building program indefinitely. That was the agreement that they had before the financial drive got underway. It was all or nothing. After the service, I saw Pastor Ed kneel at the table for a few moments. Rising from the table, he made his way back to the study. Your dad and the finance committee were meeting in an upstairs room to count the pledges. There was nothing anyone could do now but wait. Pastor Ed had challenged us with a vision for the church's future. Volunteers had worked hard to contact all the members about the dream. The campaign had been very thorough. But even so, the outcome was uncertain. You could see in his face that Pastor Ed was emotionally drained.

I knew he was worried. Several times he and your father had discussed whether or not they should have emphasized that people who already tithed were not being asked to give more. But, of course, Pastor Ed hoped everyone would give more. Let's face it, there is a core group in every church that provides most of the financial support. Without them, the church would shrivel up and disappear. Pastor Ed didn't know that Adele tithed, but he would have been very surprised if she didn't. She loves her church and she loves Christ.

I had just made it to the top of the church steps when I heard an excited knock on the pastor's door. "Pastor Ed," a voice said enthusiastically, "we made it." It was Don, the usher. "We only made it by the skin of our teeth, but we made it." "Thank God," was all I heard Pastor Ed say. "Actually our first count showed us a few hundred dollars short," Don said. "I couldn't believe it. After all that work, we weren't going to have our programs or our new building. So we counted again. And we came up with the same amount—a few hundred dollars short. I have to tell you it was like a funeral in that room. And then I happened to remember that just before the service old Mrs. Adele slipped her card into the pocket of my jacket. I guess she wasn't feeling up to coming up front. I didn't think anything of it. It fact, it had slipped my mind altogether. It was a miracle that I remembered it when I did. And, pastor, her pledge was enough to put us over the top. We did it! We did it!"

Later I found out that this happened at about the same time that Adele sat in her kitchen. Something led her to take out her Bible before making lunch. And she read the story of the widow's mite from Mark 12:41-44. She thought about Christ's words, "I tell you the truth, this poor widow has put more into the treasury than all the others. They all gave out of their wealth; but she, out of her poverty, put in everything—all she had to live on." Adele held the sacred Word in her lap for a moment. Adele asked the Lord in prayer: "Was this widow as embarrassed as I was that she had so little to give, Lord? I just hope my little bit made a difference. If it did, then that is enough."

Later Adele told me that the passage had really spoken to her. She came to understand that it's not the dollar amount that makes the difference. The difference was that her gift represented a sacrifice on her part. And that usher, Don, had it more right than he knew! It really was a miracle! It was an answer to Adele's prayer: "I just hope my little bit made a difference."

And that's the way it is in Christ's church. When everyone joins together, miracles really can and do happen. But I guess that's nothing new. I suppose that's what made the widow back in Jesus' time do what she did. Maybe her name was Adele too.

Well, I guess that's enough for now…the Hobson twins are still raising a ruckus, and Mr. Farrell still gets locked out of his house on a regular basis. Adele is helping some young mothers on the building committee pick colors for the new nursery.

Skip, when you talk to your church next time, you tell them about Mrs. Adele. They'll understand!

Love,

Mom

*(Looking up from the letter)*

Well, as you can see, I did what my mom suggested. That Adele, she's quite a woman. I wonder if she'll ever know how much she's taught others about faith?

# Other Creative Ideas for Letters From Home

• Most experienced preachers have a wealth of stories that come from personal and professional experiences. Many of these are appropriate in the context of the letter. They are frequently humorous, usually pithy, and almost always give insight into our common humanity. But remember, if it's a true story from a real experience, the names and places should be changed to protect the innocent—and the guilty!

• There are a number of books that share collections of stories or "parables" that can be incorporated into a Letter From Home. Although hard to find, the little book *The East Burlap Parables*, by Richard Rinker contains a wealth of funny and sad stories.[9] The more contemporary books *Stories I Couldn't Tell While I Was a Pastor,* by Bruce McIver[10] and *Holy Humor,* by Cal and Rose Samra[11] offer a wonderful variety of stories. Materials and stories from authors Leo Buscaglia and Max Lucado can also be fruitful resources for Letter From Home ideas.[12]

• The use of contemporary versions of the Scriptures can be effective in the letter format. Clarence Jordan's Cotton Patch series place the events of the New Testament in nineteenth-century Georgia.[13] Although paraphrases like these are not accurate from an academic standpoint, they are definitely thought provoking as they move several Bible stories into a modern context and, in doing so, confront us in our comfortable world.

PASTOR WENDELL STAVITZ FELT IT WAS IMPORTANT TO MAKE THE CONGREGATION FEEL AT HOME.

# CHAPTER 6

# The Brown Bag Sermon

# TELLING THE STORY

If there's such a thing as an affectionate nickname for a style of sermon, this one could be called Stump the Chump! From the preacher's point of view, a Brown Bag Sermon is exciting, scary, unpredictable, powerful, and sometimes nothing short of a miracle. The Brown Bag Sermon is actually a means of giving the congregation permission to ask any question, explore any issue, or seek information about any topic.

> *A preacher's desire to keep his or her preaching relevant combined with the unspoken questions about the Christian faith in the minds of some listeners, presents the perfect opportunity for what has befittingly been labeled "The Brown Bag Sermon."*

In most congregations there exist a surprising number of people who won't participate in a group Bible study because they are self-conscious about their lack of biblical knowledge. These members have sincere and honest questions but are typically afraid to ask them for fear of appearing foolish. Rather than take the risk, they remain silent and are even intimidated to study the Bible on their own. In most congregations there are also those who, if given a chance, would ask important questions about their faith and church traditions.

Also consider the all-too-frequent and sometimes justified complaint from listeners that the preaching heard from the pulpit is "not relevant to my life." If there is validity in this observation, and there frequently is, the obvious response of the preacher is, Tell me what you want to hear about. What can I give you that will help get you through your week? What is weighing on your mind and pressing your spirit?

A preacher's desire to keep his or her preaching relevant combined with the unspoken questions about the Christian faith in the minds of some listeners, presents the perfect opportunity for what has befittingly been labeled "The Brown Bag Sermon."

> *From the preacher's point of view, a Brown Bag Sermon is exciting, scary, unpredictable, powerful, and sometimes nothing short of a miracle.*

To prepare for this sermon, begin with a simple brown paper bag. Place it next to a pad of paper and some pencils at the rear of the worship area. Whenever members of the congregation have questions about their faith, a church tradition, or the Bible, encourage them to write the questions down and place them in the brown paper bag. The only rule about what questions can be asked is that "there is no rule." Any topic or issue is fair game. In a sense, the bag becomes "the place where sermons are born."

Two ways to deliver a Brown Bag Sermon are with precise preparation and clear focus or in an impromptu fashion, which definitely adds an element of excitement and challenge. I discuss both methods further in the "Delivery" section.

*Two ways to deliver a Brown Bag Sermon are with precise preparation and clear focus or in an impromptu fashion, which definitely adds an element of excitement and challenge. I discuss both methods further in the "Delivery" section.*

# CHOOSING THE TOPIC

Obviously the key to a successful Brown Bag Sermon is found in the topics to be covered as well as their presentation. It is important to stay true to the any-question-is-fair rule. But occasionally a few legitimate questions are asked that are simply not the "stuff" for a sermon in the worship setting. Some questions are best left for a classroom or small-group discussion, an evening dialogue, a church newsletter article, or other creative setting. Some questions may be too unfocused or too broad for use in a sermon. These will need to be narrowed in scope to allow for a meaningful response. Other questions may not be appropriate. A few people may use the Brown Bag Sermon as an opportunity to voice an anonymous complaint or to share an inappropriate joke.

If at all possible, however, every question should be treated as viable and honest. A question that may seem superfluous or even mean-spirited may indeed be a genuine, but poorly worded, question. The rules of common sense should dictate which ones to address in the context of a sermon.

After determining which questions are appropriate, the next step is to decide how many of them can be addressed in a single setting. In other words, is it possible to identify certain themes that promote several questions being addressed jointly? How much time should be allowed for each question? What Scriptures should be used as a foundation for each answer? Compiling, structuring, and researching satisfactory answers to the questions will provide a basis for the Brown Bag Sermon.

There is an additional concern in deciding which questions will be addressed: "Which of them will most benefit the body as a whole?" Sometimes when preparing a sermon of this nature, it becomes necessary to set priorities. That doesn't imply some of the questions aren't important. If a legitimate question is asked, and the preacher doesn't address it in one context or another, it might appear to the asker that it indeed was a silly question, not worth answering. It is up to the individual preacher to weigh each question and to prioritize the material. Questions that affect the entire fellowship, however, definitely need to be given high priority when deciding which ones will be considered first.

# SETTING THE SCENE

The Brown Bag Sermon is informal, thus the setting should be informal as well. A stool, a small table for the brown bag, a Bible, and a microphone are all that is necessary to set the stage. If the sermon is prepared in advance rather than presented extemporaneously, notes can be placed on the table or a music stand.

An informal setting will communicate several important points. First and foremost, it will indicate that the responses are from the heart of the preacher and not simply "stained glass" replies. The intimacy in the Brown Bag Sermon is often absent in other more traditional preaching approaches. It will simply feel different to the congregation.

> *An informal setting will communicate several important points. First and foremost, it will indicate that the responses are from the heart of the preacher and not simply "stained glass" replies. The intimacy in the Brown Bag Sermon is often absent in other more traditional preaching approaches. It will simply feel different to the congregation.*

# DELIVERY

As I suggested earlier, there are two basic methods to delivering a Brown Bag Sermon. I'll label them "reasonably safe" and "working without a net."

The safest way to present a Brown Bag Sermon is to collect questions over a number of weeks, select a topic or related topics from the questions received, research the issues, and present them on a preannounced date. It's reasonably safe because there is adequate time to prepare for the questions.

These sermons can be regularly scheduled, for example, on the fifth Sunday of every quarter, or they can appear somewhat randomly throughout the preaching year. They can even be tailored to fit certain holidays. For example, the Sunday before Christmas might be the perfect opportunity to address questions about the birth of Christ. Palm Sunday is a wonderful time to answer questions that have to do with the arrest, crucifixion, and resurrection of Christ. The possibilities are endless.

The Brown Bag Sermon can stand by itself or be combined with another approach such as the Letter From Home. One particularly creative approach might be to combine the Brown Bag Sermon with the Dialogue Sermon where two speakers take turns answering the same question from a slightly different angle. Whatever form the Brown Bag Sermon takes, it's important to remember that its intent is to provide honest and straightforward answers to questions raised by the congregation.

> *One particularly creative approach might be to combine the Brown Bag Sermon with the Dialogue Sermon where two speakers take turns answering the same question from a slightly different angle.*

For the courageous preachers who don't mind "working without a net," the extemporaneous approach to the Brown Bag Sermon can be very exciting and powerful. Presenting the sermon in this fashion means that the preacher will draw questions from the bag and answer them on the spot. There are a few things necessary to make this sermon work effectively. First of all, it's important that the preacher not ramble. The preacher should allow a specified amount of time to address each question. A good rule of thumb is to use between two and three minutes for each question. Of course, the nature of the question along with the total number of questions to be addressed will help dictate the time limit. If the preacher doesn't get to all the questions in a given setting, they can be saved for next time.

Presenting an extemporaneous Brown Bag Sermon should never be confused with an ill-prepared sermon. Extemporaneous preaching is both an art and a skill. It is necessary for the preacher to be somewhat quick on his or her "seat" (that is, if he or she is using a stool), and to be good at presenting thoughts in an organized and concise manner.

Prior to reading a question aloud to the congregation, the preacher should read it silently to make sure it is both understandable and appropriate. Sometimes it will be necessary to present a question in different words to state it more clearly and to narrow its focus. After the question is read aloud, the preacher can start swinging from the high wire, and the congregation will see if they have "stumped the chump."

*For the courageous preachers who don't mind "working without a net," the extemporaneous approach to the Brown Bag Sermon can be very exciting and powerful. Presenting the sermon in this fashion means that the preacher will draw questions from the bag and answer them on the spot.*

In answering questions in an extemporaneous manner, there are four general categories of responses that can be given.

The first response can be to answer the question honestly and directly.

The second possible response is "I don't know, but I'll find out"; or, "I'm not really sure, but I'll do my best to find the answer and present it the next time." The preacher has not failed when he or she admits that an answer is not known, and the congregation will appreciate the honesty. Listeners will much prefer to hear an honest "I don't know" over a collection of obscure responses that are intended to conceal that simple fact. Even preachers don't know everything, and reasonable people don't expect them to.

Please note that this second response has two parts—"I don't know" *and* "I'll find out." This statement establishes a commitment between the preacher and the congregation. Once the commitment is made to "find out," it should be honored. When the preacher has an answer to a question, he or she should share it with the congregation either through the sermon, newsletter, or another appropriate method. The success of a Brown Bag Sermon relies a great deal on the honesty and trustworthiness of the preacher. On the rare occasion that information shared turns out to be incorrect, it is important to notify the congregation of the correct information as soon as practical.

The third possible response is to begin with, "In my opinion..." or "This is strictly my opinion on the issue, but I believe..." Statements like these help differentiate between a response based on a.scriptural truth and one based purely on opinion. The preacher is not wrong to offer an opinion. In fact, many questions in the brown bag will specifically focus on the preacher's opinion. In many instances, listeners will be more interested in the preacher's opinion about an issue than in a theoretical application based on church doctrine.

This statement is important because it keeps a clear distinction between the writings of Scripture, the historic works of the church, and the opinions held by the preacher. It also gives listeners permission to disagree. If there is disagreement, there will hopefully be adequate time for continued discussion in another setting.

The fourth possible response is, "I don't believe I'll respond to this question." Sometimes questions should not be shared in a worship setting. The language may be inappropriate, the content may be intended to shock, or the question may have potential to be otherwise offensive. If possible, rephrase the question and address it as honestly as possible. Even if a particular question seems obscure or silly, it should be treated with respect.

Of course, one never knows what to expect with this type of extemporaneous sermon. I have found some very funny questions in the bag. Usually later it's revealed that these questions came from the church youth. But by attempting to answer the questions in an honest way, I discovered two things: (1) The number of planted questions decreased over time; and (2) some of the ones I thought were planted to be funny turned out to be honest questions, and the honest answers I gave were appreciated. In some cases, I have realized that a few of the questions are cries for help. Questions such as these should be answered in a caring, pastoral manner. You never know when or how the Holy Spirit will choose to work!

> *In some cases, I have realized that a few of the questions are cries for help. Questions such as these should be answered in a caring, pastoral manner. You never know when or how the Holy Spirit will choose to work!*

Prayer should surround the Brown Bag Sermon, like all others. An opening prayer for God's guidance and a concluding prayer for continued revelation establishes this sermon as part of the ongoing process in our search to understand God's Word.

# Other Creative Ideas for Brown Bag Sermons

• Invite members of the pastor's class, confirmation class, and explorer's class to present questions. These can be especially helpful to members who are interested in the same topics, but uncomfortable in asking about them.

• At the conclusion of a series of sermons, invite congregation members to write down any questions that have come up during the series.

• Invite members of the Sunday school program to write questions pertaining to materials studied in class.

• Invite the children of the congregation to ask questions about "what they most want to know about God." For additional fun, consider inviting parents or other adults to help answer them. But beware—questions from children are sometimes the toughest to answer!

• Invite the entire congregation to write questions following a tragic or unsettling event in the life of the congregation, community, or nation. Under these circumstances, a Brown Bag Sermon can provide a wonderful opportunity for healing and growth.

# CHAPTER 7

# The Congregational Conversation

# TELLING THE STORY

I magine for a moment, a popular daytime television talk show involving Christians conversing on significant life experiences—not a show that exploits the experiences of people, but one that creates an environment where Christians can share and learn from one another. If you can picture that kind of talk show you have a basic understanding of the premise behind the Congregational Conversation. Not only is such a sermon possible, but it is lots of fun for everyone.

My first Congregational Conversation as a sermon was unintentional and actually a mistake. Thankfully, it turned out to be much more productive than most of my mistakes. As a result, this method of presenting a sermon has blossomed into a meaningful and fun, if not a bit freewheeling, way to communicate God's Word.

To illustrate the effectiveness of this sermon, it's important for me to share how this particular method of sermon delivery was born by accident.

It was a dark and stormy morning (really!) one winter Sunday, the kind of day when the most appealing thing to do was to turn over, pull the covers over your head and go back to sleep. As I discovered a little while later, most of the congregation decided to do just that.

> *Imagine for a moment, a popular daytime television talk show involving Christians conversing on significant life experiences—not a show that exploits the experiences of people, but one that creates an environment where Christians can share and learn from one another. If you can picture that kind of talk show you have a basic understanding of the premise behind the Congregational Conversation.*

As the hour approached, it was obvious that attendance was going to be extremely low; we might fill the choir loft, but certainly not the sanctuary! But the faithful few finally did arrive. The worship leader and I stood at the front of the church discussing how we could modify our plan of worship to more appropriately fit our reduced numbers. Obviously, this was not the day for the grand hymns and congregational singing we had planned!

While we considered our options, a member of the congregation came up to ask a question that had been bothering her since the previous Sunday's sermon. The question was about differences in the translation between her own Bible and the one that had been used in the sermon itself. Since we were in no particular hurry to get things started that morning, we began talking about different Bible translations, where they came from, why they were different, and their relative strengths and weaknesses. As the conversation progressed, more and more of the worshippers gathered around and joined the conversation.

Some of them expressed their preferences for contemporary translations, some didn't understand the difference between a translation and a paraphrase, and others believed the only appropriate translation was the King James Version because of the "sound" of the words. (Aha! Auditory learners!) A quick dash to my study for two more translations and two parallel translations set a new focus for the day's message. The original plan of worship was scrapped as we considered the question brought by the member of the congregation, and *voila,* the Congregational Conversation was born!

It is a simple fact that people bring into worship a variety of experiences wrapped in diverse forms, from childhood memories and significant faith experiences to great wisdom gleaned from both occupational and family life. Even those people who are relatively young in their Christian faith (and age) bring a wealth of life experiences.

The Congregational Conversation allows members to share their life experiences and their wisdom as related to a particular topic. Christians can, and do, learn from each other (not just from the preacher!). This type of sermon creates an active-learning environment by inviting all worshippers to take part. To be successful, the conversation, which is typically moderated by the preacher, will be focused on a particular topic. If done properly, this type of sermon can provide a very powerful learning experience and definitely one that people will remember for a long time.

> *The Congregational Conversation allows members to share their life experiences and their wisdom as related to a particular topic. Christians can, and do, learn from each other (not just from the preacher!). This type of sermon creates an active-learning environment by inviting all worshippers to take part.*

The first time you present a sermon in this manner, you'll notice that it will be both comforting and stimulating. It will probably raise a few eyebrows and definitely raise as many questions as it answers. But most important, a Congregational Conversation will challenge participants to take ownership of God's Word in a way that few of them have ever experienced.

To help make this a sermon that is both manageable and successful, there are a few areas that need to be considered.

Without doubt the most important task for the preacher when presenting this type of sermon is to remain focused on its topic and purpose. The Congregational Conversation is different from the Brown Bag Sermon where diversity of topics might be the order of the day. The Congregational Conversation provides a relaxed atmosphere that can easily sidetrack the sermon if it is not properly moderated. So the first step in preparing this type of sermon is to choose a specific topic. If that focus gets lost or obscured during the conversation, the sermon will probably grind to a meaningless end. As long as it is kept in clear sight, however, the Congregational Conversation can be very effective.

> *The first time you present a sermon in this manner, you'll notice that it will be both comforting and stimulating. It will probably raise a few eyebrows and definitely raise as many questions as it answers. But most important, a Congregational Conversation will challenge participants to take ownership of God's Word in a way that few of them have ever experienced.*

# CHOOSING THE TOPIC

The sermon presentation will work best if the topic is shared with the congregation in advance. Imparting the information should be done in whatever manner is most effective in getting the word out to the congregation.

Although many worshippers will have opinions, informed opinions are usually more useful than off-the-cuff ones. Selecting and publicizing the topic in advance will have two helpful results. First, during the sermon itself, it will be much easier to stay focused on the topic. Second, those who choose to participate will have adequate time to prepare concrete contributions rather than relying on half-remembered stories from their past. Remember that the purpose of this type of sermon is to pool the collective wisdom of the congregation, not uninformed opinions.

In choosing a topic, it is important to take the care to identify one that will promote fruitful conversation. It is best to avoid topics that can be decided in a few words or those that have an obvious right or wrong side. Topics should be those that allow room for disagreement. The object is to challenge listeners to think deeply and arrive at their own well-informed faith decisions. Obviously, the best topics for a Congregational Conversation are those that allow for an honest and thought-provoking dialogue about the Christian faith or even about the beliefs of a particular congregation.

> *The object is to challenge listeners to think deeply and arrive at their own well-informed faith decisions. Obviously, the best topics for a Congregational Conversation are those that allow for an honest and thought-provoking dialogue about the Christian faith or even about the beliefs of a particular congregation.*

It is also important to acknowledge that some issues will not be resolved in a setting such as the one created by a Congregational Conversation. With certain topics, worshippers will find themselves caught on the horns of a dilemma; however that's part of the beauty because that's the way life is. The desired result is for listeners to grow in their faith as a result of the ideas, disagreements, and insights that are the fruit of such conversations. Hopefully, the worshippers will come away inspired, energized, and excited—not demoralized, defeated, and depressed!

This is not meant to imply that a conversation need be completely nonjudgmental. On the contrary, the purpose of the conversation is to make judgment calls when the occasion demands it. Christians generally understand that there are right and wrong choices. However, it is vital for the preacher and participants to focus on the ideas expressed, not on the people who choose to share them. It is generally acceptable to determine that an opinion is unacceptable or perhaps even wrong. It is not acceptable, however, to determine that the person who did the sharing is bad. The Congregational Conversation is a place for ideas and opinions, prejudices and wisdom to conflict; not for character assassinations or personal sparring.

Once the topic is chosen, it goes without saying that the preacher needs to invest sufficient energy into studying the topic. It's typically the preacher's job to moderate the conversation. The job of the moderator in this particular setting is to restate and refocus information when necessary and generally keep the presentation well balanced and on track. As moderator, it's also important to know the issue and be aware of any potentially sensitive areas. This will work best when the preacher is familiar with most, if not all, of the participants.

Some topics lend themselves easily to this type of sermon; others are much more difficult. Consider a conversation based upon the biblical concept of a "call." Such a conversation might begin with a look at the story of the burning bush that God used to call Moses or the light that began an epic change in the life of Paul. How are these "callings" alike? How are they different? How do we, as contemporary Christian believers receive our own call, or do we receive a call? How do these experiences affect our ministries? Some conversations, such as this one, can be started and structured very simply. Others take more time and investment. A particularly demanding sermon, for example, might focus on a particular issue of ethics and morality. Investing time and energy into the more difficult issues, however, carries the potential to sow seeds of enormous Christian growth.

The most successful Congregational Conversations are those that build on a scriptural foundation. They might be based on one particular reading, or focus on a variety of Scriptures that shed light on a single theme or topic. Topics that deal with important contemporary concerns generally lend success to this type of sermon.

*The most successful Congregational Conversations are those that build on a scriptural foundation. They might be based on one particular reading, or focus on a variety of Scriptures that shed light on a single theme or topic.*

# SETTING THE SCENE

At the beginning of a Congregational Conversation, it's important to discuss certain ground rules with the participants. These will include an invitation for everyone present to participate, the importance of keeping focused on the topic, and the preacher's role as moderator. After a congregation has experienced this type of sermon several times, explanation of the ground rules can be reduced to a minimum. But it's always better to over-inform than to under-explain!

# DELIVERY

A Congregational Conversation works best when it is a hybrid of both the traditional sermon and a television talk show. This typically means that the preacher will read the appropriate Scripture and then make a few comments or introduce a concept to help the congregation focus on a topic. Next, he or she will follow it up by asking a series of open-ended questions to get the congregation involved in the conversation.

Open-ended questions require more than a yes or no response and more than an obvious single-word answer. They are questions that challenge the listeners to think deeply and process information in light of their own experiences and knowledge. Let me provide a brief illustration. An example of a closed-ended question is "Did Joseph and Mary travel to Bethlehem in response to a decree issued by Caesar Augustus?" This question doesn't require much thinking. The answer is either yes or no. The question might challenge an individual's recall, but it doesn't call for a commitment to think about or to internally process the important issues of faith. The same basic subject can be rephrased into an open-ended question. "What would it be like to be pregnant and travel over a great distance as Mary did when she and Joseph responded to the decree issued by Caesar Agustus?" A question phrased like this calls for individuals to think about the answer in light of their personal experiences. It challenges listeners to move beyond simple recall and make decisions based on a complexity of ideals and beliefs. To fully engage the congregation in a fruitful faith-building discussion, it's important to phrase questions that confront listeners with a dilemma before providing an answer.

Before the conversation itself begins, it's important for the preacher to leave the pulpit or traditional preaching area. Moving to a "neutral" site will establish a less formal setting, and in a sense, give worshippers permission to participate in the sermon. It also allows the preacher to become a more neutral moderator rather than an authoritative figure speaking on behalf of God.

> *A Congregational Conversation works best when it is a hybrid of both the traditional sermon and a television talk show. This typically means that the preacher will read the appropriate Scripture and then make a few comments or introduce a concept to help the congregation focus on a topic. Next, he or she will follow it up by asking a series of open-ended questions to get the congregation involved in the conversation.*

The conversation works best if the preacher moves about in the worship space and uses a wireless microphone. Everyone who wishes to participate should be allowed to do so, from the youngest to the oldest. It is the moderator's responsibility to see that no one dominates the conversation. Occasionally, a moderator will encounter a member who wants to monopolize the conversation or someone who becomes overheated. On these occasions, it's important to remind the entire group of the purpose and focus of the conversation. Unfortunately, sometimes, the moderator needs to simply ignore an overly demanding participant in favor of others who haven't yet had the opportunity to speak.

# Sample Congregational Conversation

## Introduction

The following sermon titled "Judgment" was prepared and presented as a Congregational Conversation. Several Scriptural selections and meditations were selected and read by various readers prior to the sermon.

It actually begins with the preacher telling a story. It's a story that involves a significant moral dilemma. It's definitely a story that presents a challenge to today's church.

# JUDGMENT

Before we begin today's conversation, I want to tell you about a young woman named Kimberly. As you might suspect, Kimberly is not her real name, and some of the facts have been changed. But her story is very real.

Kimberly made a decision when she was eighteen to marry a man ten years older than she was. Everything went well for the first year; that is, until she discovered that she was pregnant. The day after she found out about her pregnancy was the last day that she ever saw her husband. By the time Ashley was born, Kimberly was single. The biological father was not even listed on the birth certificate.

Contrary to what may be your first impression, Kimberly is basically a good person. She is a bit wild at times and definitely a little headstrong, which is why she married against her parents' wishes in the first place. She did, however, have enough integrity to seek out the best for her daughter and enough pride not to ask for any help. Her parents were no longer a part of her life. Unfortunately, to make matters worse, Kimberly had only a high school diploma.

She started with what would optimistically be called a small efficiency apartment. Unfortunately, it was located in the worst part of town. But that was all she could afford. She was constantly afraid to leave her daughter alone even for a second for fear of the neighborhood. Hardly a day went by when there wasn't a drug deal of some kind going on outside. Many nights she could even hear nearby gunshots. In spite of all this, Kimberly did her best to hold down a full-time job. But even with a full-time job, minimum wage barely paid for her apartment and baby sitter, and it definitely left less than enough money to pay for her other monthly bills. As a proud young woman, Kimberly refused public aid, which she referred to as handouts. Her desire was to be independent and to take responsibility for herself and her daughter. She continued to be a participating member of a church which she believed was not only important for her, but for Ashley as well.

Over the last few years, Kimberly has held down a variety of jobs. Through her experiences she discovered that she enjoyed most working as a waitress. She eventually began to serve food and work as a cocktail waitress in one of the better hotels in the city. Although that might sound great, she paid a very high price to get there. And that's actually where things took a turn for the worse.

Kimberly met a man who offered to give her a job working in his bar downtown, which was much closer to her apartment. He needed her to work late evenings and into the night. These, of course, were the hours that Ashley was asleep. The schedule appealed to her because it meant she could be more a part of her daughter's life. The problem was that the bar was a topless bar, or what is commonly called a strip joint. But the pay was good and it did allow Kimberly to spend time with her daughter. Kimberly agreed to take the job on a trial basis. One thing led to another, and in a matter of weeks, Kimberly was asked to dance in the club.

Kimberly loved to dance, but was less than thrilled with the idea of dancing in that situation. Most of the girls working in the bar weren't people she even wanted to associate with. In fact, she was scared of most of them. But one of them who had become a friend encouraged her to give dancing a try. Whether or not it was a good decision, she agreed to take the new job. She found out that she was rather good as a dancer, and on a good night she could make up to four hundred dollars in tips. In fact, she worked only three nights a week and still tripled her income.

The money she earned allowed her to move into a nice little apartment in a part of town that had lawns, playgrounds, and the type of schools she wanted to send Ashley to. She paid a price however. In order to stay off public aid and to provide for her daughter, Kimberly had to continue working at the club. Her sense of self-worth was crumbling, and as a result her commitment to her daughter began to waver.

She was aware that what she was doing was considered wrong by many people, especially those in her church. It wasn't possible, however, to go back and undo the decisions she had made. She decided that she could no longer be a part of the church family, and rightly so. Once the story got out about her occupation, people in the church would make life unbearable for her and Ashley. But at the same time, Kimberly felt as though she needed the support of her church more than ever. That's when she decided to seek help.

Kimberly had all sorts of questions: Was she doing something completely wrong by dancing topless at the club? Was it better to be on welfare and live in a neighborhood that put her daughter's safety at risk, not to mention her own? Or was it better to make a "moral" sacrifice and continue dancing so she could provide for Ashley? She was confused. She was uncertain of her own worth in God's eyes. So she went to church for help. What would you say to Kimberly?

As we begin our discussion, it is important to keep the issue clear. Kimberly is basically a "good" girl trying to provide for her daughter. She is not doing anything illegal. There are no easy rely-on-the-family fixes because she's determined to succeed or fail on her own. She is very determined to stay off public assistance. There may be a time when she is able to return to school, but currently it is impossible at her income level. She desperately needs the love and support of a church family but is afraid that she will be ridiculed and ostracized when her job is discovered.

Let's begin our conversation by discussing the following questions:

• What do the Scriptures say about Kimberly's predicament?

• How do you think Jesus might respond to her?

• Where, if anywhere, is there a place for the church in this young woman's life?

• How can the church love and support Kimberly without condemnation? Or should the church condemn her?

• If the church does not condemn her, how should it deal with the member who will be quick to openly disdain Kimberly?

• If the actions of Kimberly are wrong, should she be allowed to remain in the fellowship of the congregation as long as she is employed as a topless dancer? Why or why not?

> *Consensus is not really the ultimate goal. If there is general disagreement in regard to a situation, an attempt should be made to end the conversation by summarizing the differences or specific disagreements. Whatever the outcome of the conversation, the sermon should end with an appropriate prayer.*

# Assessing the Conversation

The challenge for the preacher in this conversation is to moderate in such a way that Kimberly is not "lost" in the discussion. This is the real life of a real woman, not merely a theoretical situation.

The congregation may or may not come to a resolution during their conversation. If the congregation arrives at a general consensus, a statement of that consensus would be an appropriate way to conclude the conversation. Consensus is not really the ultimate goal. If there is general disagreement in regard to a situation, an attempt should be made to end the conversation by summarizing the differences or specific disagreements. Whatever the outcome of the conversation, the sermon should end with an appropriate prayer.

# Other Creative Ideas for the Congregational Conversation

There are several great ideas that can be developed into sermons that utilize a Congregational Conversation. Some lend themselves well to discussion; others are more difficult to work with and can be a demanding exercise in both faith and compassion. But almost any topic can work if it is based on Scripture, surrounded by prayer, and moderated in a positive and loving manner.

• Consider the situation of Annie. She is an unmarried teen who is pregnant and who may or may not receive support from the baby's father. Annie's parents want to "do the right thing." The conversation can revolve around what "the right thing" is. Since Annie's parents are no longer able to function in the role of primary caregiver, what should the response of the church be? Annie has an opportunity for education and a career. What should she do?

• Consider the situation of Stephen. He is a wealthy and powerful member of the community who only occasionally attends church. He is, however, a major contributor, and everyone knows it. Stephen has discovered that the congregation has allowed Jeb to become a member of the church. Jeb is homosexual, but that information is known only to a few, and his lifestyle doesn't make it obvious. Stephen has made it clear that Jeb's presence is unacceptable and that he is willing to do "whatever it takes" to see that Jeb is not a part of the church. This may include withdrawing his financial support, raising the issue with the governing board of the church, and even going to the local newspapers. The church leadership has approached you. What should the response of the church be? What are the congregation's priorities in a situation like this? How can the Scriptures help through the decision-making process?

• Your local congregation has decided to identify new avenues for mission work in your community. Several options have been discussed, but no one seems so have an idea how a decision should be made. Discuss the concept of discernment, or finding God's will, through Bible study, prayer, meditation, and discussion.

• Consider the relationship between church and family. What is the definition of the family? Is it the family's responsibility to support the church, or the church's responsibility to support the family? In what ways can the church provide more effective family ministry?

• Another very good conversation topic is tithing. What is tithing? Is it just an Old Testament concept, or is it also an important part of the New Testament? What would Jesus say about tithing? What is the Christian's responsibility in financially supporting the church?

• Rather than holding a conversation as an entire congregation, break everyone into smaller share groups. Give each group a question to discuss. After a specified amount of time, have a representative from each group report the outcome of their discussion to the whole congregation. Breaking down into smaller groups for discussion is a very effective learning tool. Smaller share groups are less threatening and provide a more intimate atmosphere for authentic sharing.

STRICKEN BY A SUDDEN SPELL OF LARYNGITIS, PASTOR FEGMAN SWITCHES ON THE AUTO-PASTOR.

# CHAPTER 8

# Enhancing the Sermon Through Media

# TELLING THE STORY

As I mentioned in chapter 1, the quality and use of media in our culture has changed so drastically that people have been conditioned to process information in ways differently than ever before. It's definitely an understatement to say that people have become dependent on the media. As a result of this reliance, the media may arguably be the single most useful tool for teaching in contemporary society. If this is true, there's little reason the church shouldn't use media technology to help communicate the Bible story. With careful review, it's possible to be selective and make good media choices that can serve as meaningful additions to sermons or worship services.

However, a few Christians are skeptical about the media and believe it is inherently evil and that its use in the church is destructive. Today, just like every day, Americans are bombarded, cajoled, coerced, and confronted by the media. Contrary to many opinions, broadcast media really is neutral. Television stations broadcast only what people will watch; radio stations broadcast only what people will listen to; movie theaters show only films for which people are willing to pay. And although the media is neutral, the message is most definitely not! There are both good and bad messages in contemporary media. There also exists an enormous gray area made up of confused signals, mixed messages, and trite stereotypes.

But with wise review and selection, media can enliven worship, illustrate a truth of Scripture in a modern way, or even become the basis for an entire service.

> *It's definitely an understatement to say that people have become dependent on the media. As a result of this reliance, the media may arguably be the single most useful tool for teaching in contemporary society.*

# CHOOSING AND DEVELOPING A SERMON WITH A MEDIA CLIP

As with the creation of any sermon, there are both good and bad ideas. Using media only for the sake of using it is generally a bad idea. Employing media to communicate a specific idea, to present a particular perspective, or to create a dilemma in the mind of the listener, can be a very good idea.

It's important that a preacher start by deciding why he or she wants to use media in a sermon. This can be accomplished by determining what the desired result is. Is it to present a scriptural truth in a contemporary setting? Is it to hook listeners into a particular way of thinking about something? Is it to pose a thoughtful question to listeners? Exactly what message does the preacher want to impart to the listener? Once these questions have been answered, it will be much easier to determine what to use.

*As with the creation of any sermon, there are both good and bad ideas. Using media only for the sake of using it is generally a bad idea. Employing media to communicate a specific idea, to present a particular perspective, or to create a dilemma in the mind of the listener, can be a very good idea.*

Generally the most productive form of media to use as part of a sermon is a video clip. One of my favorite clips is from the *Tonight Show* with host Jay Leno. He interviews people on the street about their biblical knowledge. The answers are both funny and revealing. At the very least, the responses provide an illustration of biblical illiteracy, a hodgepodge of religious misunderstandings, and insights into the "civil religion" of our day. This type of video clip is almost poignant enough to become a sermon by itself.

*Literally thousands of video clips can be used for sermons from television commercials and scenes from daytime soap operas to hot new full-length videos.*

The video clip of the *Tonight Show* can be used in a number of ways. Placing it at the beginning of a sermon will provide an excellent and captivating introduction that will speak volumes to the congregation. It would definitely be a thought-provoking introduction for a sermon on biblical illiteracy or a discussion about cultural views of God.

A brief excerpt from Dr. Martin Luther King's *I Have a Dream* might provide an excellent launching point for a sermon on equality, acceptance, or the power and authority of the church. A video collage of quick cuts featuring "church people" as portrayed on TV could easily become the basis for a sermon on "being in the world, but not of the world."

A collection of quick clips of preacher stereotypes culled from situation comedies, dramas, and televangelism might be used to build an image of the ministry and then contrasted with the call to ministry as described in the Bible.

Literally thousands of video clips can be used for sermons from television commercials and scenes from daytime soap operas to hot new full-length videos. With the amazing amount of media that is currently available, rarely is there a topical illustration that can't be found.

Consider the finale of *Places in the Heart,* which portrays a Communion scene with everyone in the movie, alive and dead, taking Communion together. This clip might provide a powerful opening illustration for a sermon on the Lord's Supper or salvation by grace.

Use of media in the sermon and worship, however, need not be limited only to video clips. Many traditional and contemporary songs carry powerful messages that can become wonderful sermon illustrations. A creative media idea for Advent is to blend the traditional music of Handel's *Messiah* with more contemporary renditions such as *The New Young Messiah*[14]; or my personal favorite, *Handel's Messiah: A Soulful Celebration*[15]. The message is simple; the vehicle changes, but the message remains the same.

> *Use of media in the sermon and worship, however, need not be limited only to video clips. Many traditional and contemporary songs carry powerful messages that can become wonderful sermon illustrations.*

Once a preacher begins viewing media clips with the purpose of developing a sermon, he or she will discover that sometimes an entire sermon idea will be born as a result. At other times the preacher will need to spend time researching various sources to find a clip that speaks to a particular topic. It is important to recognize, however, that just like Scripture, a media clip should not be taken out of context. Trying to prove a point by taking a thirty-second sound bite out of context is not the responsible use of media (or the pulpit for that matter). Care should be given to ensure that media clips stay true to their original message and intent.

One of the best ways to use audio or video clips on a regular basis is to organize a media illustration file. The most efficient way to do this is to keep sermon preparation in the back of your mind as you watch television and videos. Whenever a scene shows potential for use, make a note of it, and file it topically. Use the "Video Review Work Sheet" (p. 122) to help you to begin to create a media file.

*One of the best ways to use audio or video clips on a regular basis is to organize a media illustration file.*

# COPYRIGHT LAWS

I would be remiss if I ended this chapter without saying what most discerning preachers already know: The use of media is regulated by a series of rules commonly known as copyright laws. Unfortunately, the church has become one of the most casual violators of copyright laws in the land. Far too many churches have files of illegally copied music, unethically "borrowed" tapes, and copies of "pirated" software.

Copyright laws most definitely regulate the use of broadcast media. Radio programs, recorded music, television shows, and movies are all protected under the auspices of these laws. The specific permission necessary to use media in a sermon is something you'll need to determine for yourself. Permission requirements differ from company to company and with the intended use.

*The specific permission necessary to use media in a sermon is something you'll need to determine for yourself. Permission requirements differ from company to company and with the intended use.*

There are fair-use clauses that allow some materials to be used without seeking permission. Other material may be in the "public domain" and not require a copyright release. Still others may require written permission in advance. If you need to obtain permission, it can usually be done in a relatively short time by contacting the publisher, the broadcaster, or the production company. Written permission to use a particular work is usually easy to obtain and is often as simple as making a phone call and receiving a fax.

The Motion Picture Licensing Corporation has secured and maintains copyright releases on specific video titles. If you are a member of that organization, you are entitled to certain usage benefits on specified videos. For more information about the benefits of MPLC, contact them at 5455 Centinela Avenue, Los Angeles, CA 90066-6970 (310) 822-8855.

The word here is simply to be ethically responsible and make sure you are familiar with the copyright laws before using media in worship.

# Other Creative Ideas for Enhancing the Sermon Through Media

• As a variation to showing a clip and then launching into a traditional sermon, try asking several open-ended questions to engage the congregation in a discussion about the video scene.

• A short edited video clip from the church's youth workcamp will tell more about the experience than can be described in twice the amount of time.

• For a church anniversary celebration, consider using slides of old newspaper articles and photographs.

• For a sermon about responsible community outreach, consider presenting a short video of an interview with the director of a local mission.

• News clips from war-torn or disaster areas around the world can provide powerful illustrations for a variety of sermon topics.

PASTOR LOU BARNSLEY TRIES TO WIN BACK MEMBERS THAT HE HAD LOST TO TV PREACHERS.

# VIDEO REVIEW WORK SHEET

Title: _____

Topic: _____

Overview of clip:

_____

_____

_____

_____

Approximate start time: _____

Start cue: _____

Approximate end time: _____

End cue: _____

Possible uses:

_____

_____

_____

_____

Potential Scriptures:

_____

_____

_____

_____

# CHAPTER 9

# Other Sermon-Enhancing Ideas

There is a wide variety of other innovative ideas that can help the preacher enhance the sermon and effectively communicate the Bible story. Some are old and some are new, but several definitely deserve comment.

# THE GIANT CHILDREN'S SERMON

Most preachers regularly present a children's sermon as part of the worship service. Many who do can recount times adult members have said how much they enjoyed the children's sermon and had got a lot out of it. In fact, if those preachers were to admit it, they could probably tell stories about worshippers learning more from the children's sermon than they did from the regular sermon. There is little reason that the same techniques used to reach participants in the children's sermon can't be incorporated into the traditional sermon.

The first element of most successful children's sermons is that the message is simple and has a single focus. Furthermore, the sermon calls for interaction with the kids. Sometimes questions are asked that challenge them to consider a point and respond verbally.

One of the most effective tools used in the children's sermon is the "object lesson." In this context, the object is something such as a toy or a household item to which the kids can relate. The lesson itself develops as the preacher connects the item to an important faith lesson. It might be as simple as passing around a globe and talking about mission work or caring for people from faraway lands. An object lesson could be as simple as using a hammer to discuss Jesus' early occupation as a carpenter and how it prepared him for later events in his life. Ideas for object lessons are endless.

Children's sermons are effective because they are simple, fun, and get kids actively involved in the lesson itself. The same techniques can be applied to the traditional sermon. Asking worshippers to think about and respond to a simple open-ended question or two can enhance any sermon. Or, perhaps, providing each worshipper with a bandage while speaking about Christ's sacrifice and how "by his wounds you have been healed."

Several very helpful resources that provide creative ways to use object lessons and will help actively involve listeners in the sermon are available from Group Publishing. These include *FaithWeaver Children's Messages 1, 5-Minute Messages for Children, Bore No More!,* and *Bore No More 2.*

> *There is little reason that the same techniques used to reach participants in the children's sermon can't be incorporated into the traditional sermon.*

# THE PAGEANT

When many church members hear the word "pageant," they think of memories of small, excited children wearing angel wings and bathrobes. Unfortunately, the pageant has fallen out of favor for many churches over the years. This is most unfortunate because the pageant is a method of communication that reaches all types of learners.

A pageant is typically more involved than a drama or a skit. It often involves an elaborate entrance or parade, includes singing, and is surrounded by as much pomp as possible. The wonderful part of a pageant is that it gives children an opportunity to participate in worship or as part of the sermon.

The pageant has a long and honorable history, dating back to at least the time of St. Francis of Assisi. St. Francis sought a means to tell stories of the Christian faith to those that couldn't read. He chose to do so by means of small vignettes, or what we would call a pageant. These "little plays" emphasized telling Bible stories in a manner that could be seen, heard, and experienced by the audience.

> *St. Francis sought a means to tell stories of the Christian faith to those that couldn't read. He chose to do so by means of small vignettes, or what we would call a pageant. These "little plays" emphasized telling Bible stories in a manner that could be seen, heard, and experienced by the audience.*

The pageant provides an opportunity for the congregation to focus on a particular Bible story or theme. Whether the costuming is elaborate or simple, the setting historic or contemporary, the pageant is a creative opportunity to draw listeners into the Bible story. Reenactments of the Nativity, the Last Supper, Jesus' triumphal entry into Jerusalem, the receiving of the Holy Spirit on Pentecost, the Red Sea crossing, and Noah's ark are excellent stories upon which pageants can be based.

In their most inclusive form, pageants provide an opportunity to involve every member of the congregation in the story. For example, a reenactment of the triumphal entry of Jesus can involve every spectator, shouting and crying, and processing into the worship area waving palm branches. A reenactment of the Sermon on the Mount or receiving of the Holy Spirit might involve every worshipper. Only creativity and the logistics of a particular location are limiting factors in putting on a pageant.

Several wonderful children's pageants are available from Group Publishing in their Instant Christmas Pageant series: *The Fumbly Bumbly Angels, The Not-So-Silent Night,* and the recently released *Wee Three Kings.*

# SKITS

Skits are closely related to pageants, but are generally less elaborate in their production. A typical skit is four to seven minutes in length. The sole purpose for using a skit as part of the sermon is to introduce a topic, event, character, or dilemma. A number of good skit resource providers are Willow Creek Church, Contemporary Drama Services, Group Publishing, and the Covenant Players. All provide scripts at a reasonable price.

> *The beauty of a skit is that it includes elements that speak to listeners of all three learning styles. If a skit is included as a regular part of the sermon, the preacher can be more assured that he or she is providing an effective learning environment for the congregation.*

It is not always necessary to purchase a book or script. The average congregation has at least a few members who with a little practice can become skilled at the art of improvisational acting. Improvisational acting means to compose and perform a skit or drama with little preparation. A skit performed in this manner can be an exciting and powerful part of any sermon. Although improvisational acting is a skill which takes practice to master, with a little direction, practice, and interest, volunteers can become quite accomplished at performing improvisational skits. A small congregational drama group, if given a topic and a little advance warning, can usually produce an energetic skit that is both creative and practical.

The beauty of a skit is that it includes elements that speak to listeners of all three learning styles. If a skit is included as a regular part of the sermon, the preacher can be more assured that he or she is providing an effective learning environment for the congregation.

As with anything new, start small. Two volunteer performers, a chair or a stool for scenery, a couple of props, and an attention-grabbing topic are all that is necessary. A simple skit is an exciting way to launch any sermon.

While there are many good skit books available, *High-Impact Worship Dramas* by John Duckworth is loaded with powerful skits from creative parables to TV-show parodies. Duckworth's skits will definitely add life to any sermon. The book is available from Group Publishing under the Vital Ministry imprint.

*The average congregation has at least a few members who with a little practice can become skilled at the art of improvisational acting. A skit performed in this manner can be an exciting and powerful part of any sermon.*

# DRAMATIC INTERPRETATION

Dramatic interpretation falls somewhere between a dramatic reading and a skit or a drama. It provides a simple and powerful way to share a dramatic presentation with less time investment than a regular drama. The dramatic interpretation typically involves one or two people wearing regular street clothes, and taking on specific reading roles. The script is not memorized, but is spoken from notebooks carried by the performers.

In some ways the dramatic interpretation is like the Dialogue Sermon because it is a shared reading. But it goes beyond that by employing the use of motion and movements. For example, the readers might pace back and forth as they read, change locations, and make other specified movements with their hands or bodies.

The dramatic interpretation definitely has several advantages over other forms of drama. Since it is performed from a script, it doesn't require the preparation time of other dramatic pieces. Neither does it require the use of costuming or props, and there is no need of transition time between the presentation and the rest of the sermon. Besides that, a dramatic interpretation is less intimidating for the novice.

Scripts for the dramatic interpretation can come from almost any source. It can be a selection of poetry, history, or a dramatic selection of prose. Timing, pacing, inflection of voice, and the motion of the body are all tools to convey words and meanings through this form of communication. Consider, for example, Robert Frost's poem "The Road Not Taken." As the actor reads about looking down a path, he or she might pause for a moment as though looking somewhere far away. As the actor reads about traveling down a path, he or she might walk as though it's actually occurring. The movements are generally very simple, but add an incredible amount of emotional energy to the reading. The dramatic interpretation can effectively be used either at the beginning or the end of a sermon depending on the desired effect.

*In some ways the dramatic interpretation is like the Dialogue Sermon because it is a shared reading. But it goes beyond that by employing the use of motion and movements. For example, the readers might pace back and forth as they read, change locations, and make other specified movements with their hands or bodies.*

# DRAMA

Although the large drama is beyond the scope of this book, it does at least deserve mention. There are a number of excellent dramatic works that are quite effective in supporting the sermon and otherwise becoming part of the worship service. Dramatic or humorous, musical or traditional, large cast or small, theatrical pieces are excellent tools for teaching. Although large dramas take a considerable amount of work to do properly, the time is usually well spent, and the production definitely becomes a gift for the congregation.

There are numerous dramatic pieces available for church use from a variety of sources.

# CLOWNING, PUPPETS, AND DANCE

There is a wide variety of specialized ministries that can add depth to the worship service and sermon. These include clowning ministries, puppet ministries, and liturgical dance teams. If done properly, these creative communication methods can enliven a worship service or sermon. Poorly executed, however, they can become a distraction.

**Clowning.** There are times when the freedom of a clown allows worshippers to step outside themselves for a few moments and gain a different kind of perspective. Clowning challenges worshippers to laugh at their own foibles, gain special insight into particular topics, and take a relaxing break from the routine of their week. Those who are familiar with clown ministries will generally affirm that adding an element of clowning to the worship service can be very healing and will touch the hearts of worshippers in unique ways.

*Clowning challenges worshippers to laugh at their own foibles, gain special insight into particular topics, and take a relaxing break from the routine of their week.*

**Puppets.** Puppets have a long history in the life of the church, going back as far as the middle ages. Even though puppets are typically thought of as appealing only to children, if given an opportunity, they will definitely add an exciting depth to the traditional sermon.

The strength of a puppet comes from its ability to paint stereotypical pictures of the people we meet in the world around us. Good or evil, simple or wise, the voice of each puppet is allowed to speak of vice or virtue in a manner that is non-threatening to listeners. An effective puppet ministry can speak to issues that would otherwise be difficult to approach in the context of a traditional sermon. Just like a skit, a puppet presentation can be used to effectively open or close a sermon.

*The strength of a puppet comes from its ability to paint stereotypical pictures of the people we meet in the world around us. Good or evil, simple or wise, the voice of each puppet is allowed to speak of vice or virtue in a manner that is nonthreatening to listeners.*

**Dance.** Dance, or what is commonly referred to as liturgical dance, is another element of communication that can be either a blessing or a distraction. The idea of dance as a part of worship has been around at least since King David, so it's nothing new. If the truth were known, every form of worship includes an element of dance. Whether it is the simple movements associated with the progression of the worship service, the formalized movements of processionals and recessionals, or the liturgical movements associated with High Mass, dance is a very real part of worship. Liturgical dance is a tool of expression and communication that takes the normal movement of worship a step further. It definitely has elements that appeal to all three learning styles. Liturgical dance is typically choreographed to an appropriate musical piece and if done properly can be a very powerful means of communication. Liturgical dance is not that much different than a drama. But rather than communicating through words, participants communicate through motion and movement. It can be as simple as a dance that brings elements of the Lord's Supper to the front of the worship area or as complex as a reenactment of Jesus' journey along the road to Golgotha.

*Liturgical dance is not that much different than a drama. But rather than communicating through words, participants communicate through motion and movement.*

# LEARNING BY CELEBRATING ETHNIC DIVERSITY

Since its inception, part of the rich heritage of the Christian faith has been a rich diversity in the body of believers. From the earliest "discussions" between Peter and Paul regarding the proper inclusion of Gentiles in the church, Christians have been bringing their unique talents, songs, and traditions to lay as offerings at the foot of the cross.

It's a rare congregation today that does not represent some ethnic diversity. The worship service provides many wonderful opportunities to extol God's diverse creation.

The music and traditions of various nationalities can be creatively blended together to affirm and celebrate ethnic diversity in worship. A special day, set aside to lift up a particular ethnic group, provides opportunities for worshippers to learn about the heritage of fellow Christians, and it provides new stimulus for the eyes, ears, and heart.

> *A special day, set aside to lift up a particular ethnic group, provides opportunities for worshippers to learn about the heritage of fellow Christians, and it provides new stimulus for the eyes, ears, and heart.*

Take, for example, the Christian Church (Disciples of Christ) which is a descendent of the Presbyterian Church of Scotland. Two of its important founders were Scotch-Irish and brought not only their faith to America, but also many of the Celtic traditions that were part of their lives. To celebrate the heritage of the Christian Church movement many local churches set a day aside for a "Kirkin' o' the Tartans." The day includes Scottish country dancing, pipers, kilts, Scottish Christian hymns, bread puddings, scones, and shortbread. Not only does a celebration like this provide a meaningful and fun diversion from the normal worship service, but it also allows for new experiences in the context of the Christian faith. This heritage day provides an opportunity for a creative sermon such as a dramatic interpretation based on "The Deer's Cry" (commonly known as "St. Patrick's Breastplate") or a Letter From Home from "Cousin Patrick." A celebration like this will definitely be one that will not soon be forgotten.

NEW PASTOR RALPH MUMFORD HAD HIS WORK CUT OUT FOR HIM.

# CHAPTER 10

# Considerations for Effective Preaching and Worship

# EVALUATING THE WHOLE WORSHIP EXPERIENCE

S o far this book has presented ideas that will help engage worshippers in the sermon and release their conditioned ears to hear God's Word in a new way. But why stop with just the sermon? Why not incorporate active experiences into other parts of the worship service? Jesus taught through experiences that engaged all the senses and King David demonstrated spontaneous, creative worship on the streets of Jerusalem; we definitely have many biblical examples of teaching and worship that call for active participation.

Some churches have formalized liturgical services, while other traditions have informal services of worship. In either circumstance and in anything in between, elements of active participation can be brought in. Prior to making wholesale changes in worship, however, it's important to understand the needs of each congregation. Of course, understanding partly comes with recognizing the differences between learning styles and acknowledging the need for a variety of approaches in worship.

*Small changes that incorporate elements of active involvement into worship will typically gain tremendous ground. Most congregations can adapt to fairly minor modifications in the worship service, and these modifications will accomplish wonders.*

Making immediate major changes is not generally advisable, unless a congregation has reached a point where there is nothing to lose. Changing something simply for the purpose of change is not a good reason for doing so. Small changes that incorporate elements of active involvement into worship will typically gain tremendous ground. Most congregations can adapt to fairly minor modifications in the worship service, and these modifications will accomplish wonders.

Consider for a moment some very minor alterations in the reading of Scripture that will encourage the congregation to become more actively involved without interrupting the natural flow of worship. For example, involve the congregation in the reading of Scripture, rather than having the preacher do this single-handedly. The congregation might read verses aloud together or read them responsively with the leader. Or the leader might read verses of Scripture while the congregation responds between each verse by singing a short chorus or a verse set to music. Another creative way to read Scripture is to assign several readers ahead of time who will be seated in different parts of the worship area. When it's time for the Scripture reading, they can stand and read their assigned passages from their places in the congregation.

Even something as simple as the preacher or worship leader moving to a new location to read the Scripture can add a creative element. For example, picture the impact of the words of John the Baptist proclaiming, "Make straight the way for the Lord" as the words come from the *back* of the worship area. Or consider the congregational response while it listens to the pastor's words as he or she reads Scripture while walking throughout the worship area. Or imagine the visual and kinesthetic differences in the worship experience if a preacher reads a psalm while standing directly in front of the congregation facing the cross. Even these simple changes can have an exciting impact on the quality of the worship service.

*Imagine the visual and kinesthetic differences in the worship experience if a preacher reads a psalm while standing directly in front of the congregation facing the cross. Even these simple changes can have an exciting impact on the quality of the worship service.*

Celebrating the Lord's Supper can become a more powerful and meaningful experience with only slight modifications. Consider, for example, the tremendous symbolism portrayed if the bread and the cup are brought forward as part of the offering rather than having them set out on a table beforehand. Or during the Thanksgiving season, a congregation might decorate the front of the worship area with a traditional cornucopia surrounded by an abundance of family gifts such as produce, home-canned goods, crafts, and artistic creations. Then during the worship, the bread and cup are lifted from among this bounty and celebrated as the most wonderful of all gifts. It will present a powerful image to the worshippers.

*To get children more involved in this worship experience, consider having them decorate paper grocery bags to be handed out a couple of weeks before a food offering is taken. Imagine the thrill of the children as they help adult worshippers bring the bags full of food forward during a special dedication.*

Most churches collect food or canned goods as part of a community outreach program. But rather than stacking the food items in an out-of-the-way place, invite participants forward during the service to offer their contributions as acts of worship and dedication. Invite musicians to play a lively selection of music while the joyful chaos of worshippers come forward with their offerings; young people could assist those who aren't able to make the trip. Visual processors will be overwhelmed and delighted by the movement, auditory processors will be inundated with the cacophony of sound, and kinesthetic processors will appreciate the drama!

To get children more involved in this worship experience, consider having them decorate paper grocery bags to be handed out a couple of weeks before a food offering is taken. Imagine the thrill of the children as they help adult worshippers bring the bags full of food forward during a special dedication.

Consider how the choir might inspire the congregation to participate in deeper, more meaningful worship. Does the choir sit in a choir loft or in the front of the worship area? Perhaps, for one particular service, they could sit with families and friends and sing from where they are seated or begin to sing an anthem as they slowly emerge from the congregation and come forward.

*Consider how the choir might inspire the congregation to participate in deeper, more meaningful worship. Does the choir sit in a choir loft or in the front of the worship area? Perhaps, for one particular service, they could sit with families and friends and sing from where they are seated or begin to sing an anthem as they slowly emerge from the congregation and come forward.*

There are other parts of worship that lend themselves very nicely to creativity and active participation. Prayer, for example, can become a more personal experience by having worshippers join together in small groups or pairs to share their concerns and joys and then pray for each other. Or maybe the ushers could hand out pencils and slips of paper to participants as the preacher invites each person to write down a prayer concern. Afterward, everyone could be invited forward to help make a "prayer collage" by taping his or her concern on a piece of poster board. Even though some of these ideas require more preparation and time, the resulting powerful experiences and memories are typically worth the extra effort.

Making worship a more memorable experience by adding elements of creativity need not be elaborate, expensive, or time consuming. Even the smallest change can add excitement and meaning to the worship experience.

# LOGISTICAL CONSIDERATIONS FOR PREACHING

No matter how innovative the preacher has been in developing a creative worship experience and meaningful sermon, the desired results will fall short if technical and logistical problems aren't addressed. It goes without saying that the best sermon will fail if the listeners can't hear or see the preacher. Garbled words, poor amplification, and sound distortions make it difficult for the listeners to concentrate on a message or presentation.

> *No matter how innovative the preacher has been in developing a creative worship experience and meaningful sermon, the desired results will fall short if technical and logistical problems aren't addressed.*

Long before the sermon is ever delivered, certain conditions need to be assessed in the worship area and, if necessary, corrected. As obvious as it seems, simple questions need to be asked: Is the preaching area visible from all areas of the worship setting? Are there certain places on the platform or near the front of the worship area that are obstructed from certain viewers? Is the amplification system adequate? How about those worshippers whose hearing has diminished or is impaired?

Many preachers either don't think about these things or assume there is no problem. All of these are important issues, especially as the preacher or speaker begins moving to nontraditional places throughout the worship area. For example, if the sermon is presented as a Letter From Home, the pastor will sit in a comfortable chair beside a small table. But if the presentation is obstructed from the view of a third of the listeners, the message will lose its full effect. Similarly, if some of the worshippers can't hear because the preacher has moved away from the stationary microphone, the message might just as well be falling on deaf ears.

The easiest place to begin is with a survey of the room itself. Visit the sanctuary during the week when it is empty. Move about the room, sitting in several different locations. If preaching plans include moving around on the platform or down onto floor level, areas need to be identified that might potentially be obstructed from a clear view. If a problem is identified, correction might be as simple as rethinking a specific movement or setting, or it may involve improving the basic layout of the worship area. Some problems may be easy to correct, while others may present significant challenges. But, at least, awareness will allow the worship service to be designed to minimize potential problems for worshippers.

*Whether or not preaching plans include moving about the worship area for creative sermon presentations, it's definitely worth the effort to be aware of potential visibility problems.*

Recently I witnessed a worship service that involved a dramatic monologue where the presenter dropped to the floor and completed his presentation lying down. The preacher wasn't even visible from where I sat in the eighth row. The worshippers seated behind me could not possibly have seen what was happening. What had promised to be a wonderful and moving sermon lost its effect because the presentation wasn't thought through ahead of time.

One rule of thumb in the theater is, If you can't see the audience, the audience can't see you! It's a rule that is very important for the preacher who begins incorporating creative movement into sermon presentations. It's always advisable for the preacher to practice his or her presentation from the exact location where it will be presented. If every seat isn't visible, the sermon will lose its impact.

Whether or not preaching plans include moving about the worship area for creative sermon presentations, it's definitely worth the effort to be aware of potential visibility problems.

*One rule of thumb in the theater is, If you can't see the audience, the audience can't see you! It's a rule that is very important for the preacher who begins incorporating creative movement into sermon presentations.*

Just as important as assessing the visibility of the worship area is checking for potential sound problems. Again, this should be done when the worship area is quiet. The easiest way to assess the effectiveness of the sound system is to play a selection of music over the system and move about the room. Can it be heard clearly from every location? If there are dead spots, it may not necessarily indicate that the sound system is inadequate. Sound is affected by surfaces; hard surfaces reflect sound better than soft ones. For example, wood floors make for a more lively, or brighter, sound. Carpeting has a tendency to deaden sound. There are many ways to correct sound problems short of purchasing a new system.

> *The importance of an adequate sound system for preaching and worship cannot be overemphasized. The preacher may use all types of creative presentations in worship, but even the best efforts will be ineffective if participants have difficulty hearing.*

An additional consideration when assessing sound amplification needs is to determine whether or not the congregation has members who are hearing impaired. If so, there are several wonderful wireless hearing systems that will make them feel that they, too, are an important part of the worship service.

If the chosen course of action, however, is to purchase a new sound system, it should be done only after careful assessment of the congregation's current and future needs. As part of the assessment, it's imperative that a professional sound technician be consulted. There is a substantial difference in choosing a sound system for worship and choosing one for the home.

The importance of an adequate sound system for preaching and worship cannot be overemphasized. The preacher may use all types of creative presentations in worship, but even the best efforts will be ineffective if participants have difficulty hearing. The sound system is definitely not the place to cut corners when the central focus is to communicate the Bible story!

"I'M HOPING THESE NEW SPEAKERS WILL GIVE MY SERMONS A LITTLE MORE PUNCH."

# A Final Thought

A FINAL THOUGHT

Communicating the Bible story is an ongoing task that must continually take new shape as the world changes around us. The Bible teaches that the story never changes, but life teaches that the way it is presented must always change. It's really perplexing to think about. Although the message is as ancient as Creation and as dramatic as the Resurrection, it must also be as fresh as the breath of a newborn babe. Presenting the Bible story is a high calling for those who have accepted the challenge; it's a task that produces both excitement and fear at the same time.

Speaking to the hearts and minds of people is certainly much too important to be limited by the ideas presented in this book. Thus it is my hope that these pages will spark new forms of creativity in the minds of all those who have chosen to read it.

Blessings to you as you continue inviting listeners to encounter God's Word so they themselves become the light of that Word.

# Endnotes

## Foreword by Leonard Sweet

1. See Eberhard Jungel's thesis in *God as the Mystery of the World: On the Foundation of the Theology of the Crucified One in the Dispute Between Theism and Atheism,* trans. Darrell L. Guder (Grand Rapids, MI: William B. Eerdmans Publishing Co., 1983), 11, where he writes: "The art of speaking does not result in something different from itself; instead, its effect consists of the fact that the person addressed and the result of what is said are both drawn into the act of speaking." Jungel calls this a "perlucutionary-attractive act."

2. Bernice Kanner, "hungry, Or jut Boree?" American Demographics 21 (January 1999), 15. The survey was conducted by Cyber Dialogue, New York City, August 1998.

3. Ryan MacPherson, "Show and Tell," Preacher's Magazine, 71 (June/August 1996), 13-15.

4. Charles Sanders Pierce's greatest work is preserved in a collection of posthumously published essays: *Chance, Love, and Logic: Philosophical Essays,* ed. Morris R. Cohen (New York: Harcourt, Brace and World, 1923; reprint, Barnes and Noble, 1968).

5. For more see my *SoulTsunami: Sink or Swim in New Millennium Culture* (Grand Rapids, MI: Zondervan Press, 1999), chapter 6. For the Web version see http://www.soulsunami.com/section6.h (Grand Rapids, MI: Zondervan, 1999).

## Chapters 1–10

1. Two favorites of mine are works by fellow Disciples preacher Fred Craddock, *As One Without Authority* (Haymaker Press, 1971); and *Preaching* (Nashville, TN: Abingdon Press, 1985). These works provide a solid basis for developing a sermon, both in style and content.

2. There are several excellent books that provide an overview of women in the Bible: Ruth Tucker and Walter Liefeld, *Daughters of the Church: Women in Ministry From New Testament Times to the Present,* (Grand Rapids, MI: Zondervan, 1987); Edith Deen, *All of the Women of the Bible* (Harper and Row, 1983); Denise Lardner Carmody's, *Biblical Women* (Crossroads, 1992); and a collection of monologues by Mary Jensen titled *Women of the Bible Tell Their Stories* (Minneapolis, MN: Augsburg Publishing House, 1978).

3. The book by the Reverend James Ryan, *Conversations With God* (St. Louis, MO: Christian Board of Publications, 1984) is excellent for studying and developing this particular sermon style.

4. The Jewish Passover ceremony Haggadah includes specific questions and answers as part of the service. The questions are asked by the youngest participant and the answers are provided by the table host. See a copy of the *Passover Haggadah* for a more complete understanding of this ritual. Two other interesting books that focus on the Passover as a part of the developing Christian tradition are *Passover Haggadah: A Messianic Celebration,* by Eric-Peter Lipson, JFJ Press, 1986, and *Christ in the Passover: Why Is This Night Different?* by Ceil and Moishe Rosen, 1978, Moody Press, Chicago.

5. "Where Is God?" was written for delivery at First Christian Church in Cheyenne, Wyoming, for Holocaust Sunday, 1998. The author, Roger McDaniel, is presently a seminarian and candidate for ordination. This material was used with his permission.

6. Elie Wiesel, *Night* (Bantam Doubleday, 1960).

7. Garrison Keillor's stories from Lake Woebegon have been featured as part of the National Public Radio show *A Prairie Home Companion* and can be found in recorded form as well as in print.

8. The idea for this Letter From Home came from a sermon prepared by King Duncan and distributed through Seven Worlds.

9. Richard Rinker, *The East Burlap Parables* (Lincoln, NE: University of Nebraska Press, 1969).

10. Bruce McIver, *Stories I Couldn't Tell While I Was a Pastor* (Carmel, NY: Guideposts Press, 1991).

11. Cal and Rose Samra, *Holy Humor* (Carmel, NY: Guideposts Press, 1996). The Joyful Noiseletter is a wonderful resource containing a wealth of funny material and provides a copyright lease (for local use only) with every issue. They may be contacted at Fellowship of Merry Christians, P.O. Box 895, Portage, MI 49081-0895, or http://www.joyfulnoiseletter.com.

12. As with any copyrighted material, appropriate credit should be given. I maintain a list of any copyrighted materials used in a sermon and keep the list on file. Full copyright information, such as publisher and date, need not be included in the actual sermon presentation.

13. Clarence Jordan, *The Cotton Patch Version of Matthew and John* (Chicago, IL: Association Press, Follett Publishing Company, 1970). There are also Cotton Patch versions of Paul's Epistles as well as Luke and Acts.

14. *The New Young Messiah*, The Sparrow Corporation, P.O. Box 5010, Brentwood, TN, 1993.

15. *Handel's Messiah: A Soulful Celebration*, Reprise Records, Time Warner Corp., 3300 Warner Blvd., 1993.